Style Investing

WILEY FRONTIERS IN FINANCE
Edited by Edward I. Altman

Damodaran on Valuation: Security Analysis for Investment and Corporate Finance
    Aswath Damodaran (Book / Disk set also available)

Study Guide for Damodaran on Valuation: Security Analysis for Investment and Corporate Finance
    Aswath Damodaran

Valuation: Measuring and Managing the Value of Companies, Second Edition
    Tom Copeland, Tim Koller, and Jack Murrin
    (Book / Disk set also available)

Financial Statement Analysis, Second Edition
    Martin S. Fridson

Style Investing: Unique Insight Into Asset Allocation
    Richard Bernstein

The Stock Market, 6th Edition
    Richard J. Teweles, Edward S. Bradley, and Ted M. Teweles

Fixed Income Securities: Tools for Today's Markets
    Bruce Tuckman

Style Investing

Unique Insight Into Equity Management

Richard Bernstein

John Wiley & Sons, Inc.
New York • Chichester • Brisbane • Toronto • Singapore

Copyright © 1995 by John Wiley & Sons, Inc.
Published by John Wiley & Sons, Inc.

Library of Congress Cataloging-in-Publication Data:

Bernstein, Richard, 1958–
    Style investing : Unique insight into equity management / Richard Bernstein.
        p.   cm.
    ISBN 0-471-03570-X (acid-free paper)
    1. Investment analysis.   2. Market segmentation.   I. Title.
    II. Title: Style investing.
    HG4529.B466   1995
332.6—dc20   94-35163

Printed in the United States of America

10 9 8 7 6 5 4 3 2 1

To Chris and my parents

Acknowledgments

There are many people who have contributed to this book in one way or another. First, I must thank two of my long-time coworkers at Merrill Lynch, Satya Pradhuman and Joan Christensen. One will see Satya's name so often in the references at the end of each chapter that I am sure he will soon be asking for royalties, and I believe Joan's superb research assistance is unparalleled on the Street. In addition, I should thank Bernie Tew, my coauthor on several journal articles, and Andrea White, his research assistant (and wife). Whenever we write papers together, it seems as though they do all the dirty work. The newer members of Merrill's Quantitative Analysis Department deserve thanks as well: Markus Barth and Wendy Misik.

Other of my colleagues at Merrill Lynch who have contributed to this book, often without realizing it and sometimes just by making a casual comment that started my research in a new direction, are: Joe Belfatto, Steve Bodurtha, Don Bronstein, Chuck Clough, Anne Cox, Bob Davis, Bob Farrell, Marty Fridson, Lee Gatewood, Paul Galietto, Bill Gordon, Jamie Greenwald, Dick Hardy, David Horner, Richard Klein, Andy Melnick, Eric Mitofsky, Chuck Mooser, Jack Roehrig, Bruce Steinberg, Cheryl Van Winkle, Tom White, and Arthur Zeikel. I am greatly indebted to the entire institutional equity sales force at Merrill Lynch for the exposure that I now have among our client base. In addition, I especially thank Jack Lavery and Jerry Kenny, who seem to have endless faith in me, and in my groups' abilities to develop new and insightful research products. My thanks also to George Nitchelm, Barbara Fiegenbaum, Jean Cockroft, and Jack Kavanaugh of Merrill Lynch Research Compliance, who have always managed to keep me out of trouble. Former colleagues who have impacted this work include: Jeff Applegate, Bob Barbera, Tim Sargent, and Stan Shipley.

Several academicians who have helped me tremendously are Ed Altman (who convinced me to write this book) of the NYU Stern School of Business, Larry Harris of USC, and Meir Statman of Santa Clara University. One professor deserves special thanks: Rick Werner, a philosophy professor at Hamilton College. The minicourse I took with Rick in 1979 on Relativity has had a greater impact on my financial research than any other course I have ever taken.

There are hundreds of clients that I should thank individually for helpful comments A few deserve special mention: Sandip Baghat (TIMCO), Ken Barker (Mellon Equity Associates), Dan Bukowski (Kemper), Dan Cardell (Continental Illinois), Dan Coggin (Media General), Jeff Diermeier (Brinson Partners), John Fields and Bernie Schafer (Delaware Management), Tony Elavia (Piper Capital Management), Bruce Fielitz (Atlanta Capital), Dick Holcomb (State of Michigan), Jean Ledford (State of Wisconsin), Rob Parenteau (RCM), Don Peters (T. Rowe Price), Steve Soames (State Street Research), Judy Studer (GE Investments), John Wightkin (Ohio State Teachers), and David Upshaw (Waddell & Reed), Sometimes I think this group forgets that it is supposed to be the "sell" side, which gives investment insights to the "buy" side, and not the other way around.

All of those mentioned were tremendously generous with their help in one form or another. However, any mistakes or omissions are purely my fault.

RICHARD BERNSTEIN

Preface

*F*ormal market segmentation and style investing have become an integral part of asset management over the past ten to twenty years. The advent of the pension consultant has forced both money managers and plan sponsors to pay particular attention to equity market segment and investment style exposures. More recently, competition within the mutual fund industry has led to the development of funds that invest solely in unique market segments or follow particular styles.

The problem confronting many investment professionals is that true market segments, by definition, will not all perform similarly. Pension plan sponsors and, with the growth of defined contribution plans and 401(k)s, individuals must now decide not only whether to allocate assets to stocks or bonds, but also to growth, value, income, small capitalization, and large capitalization equity, just to name a few.

Anecdotal history suggests that it is difficult to actively time the performance of different market segments. Investors and pension plan sponsors have historically tended to reallocate funds toward successful segment or style-oriented money managers as the particular money manager's style outperforms. The urgency to reallocate funds grows as the particular style continues to outperform, until the maximum allocation favoring the particular style occurs at the style's performance peak. Similarly, start-up money management firms will tend to follow the latest outperforming investment theme.

This book attempts to highlight the macroeconomic, microeconomic, and expectational factors that can affect equity market segment performance. In general, most segments can be simplified to those perceived to be "safe" or "risky" at any point in time, and investors have historically rotated from those perceived to be risky to those perceived to be safe. Expectational analysis, however, generally demonstrates that overwhelming acceptance of a particular investment style or theme or, in other words, the overwhelming acceptance that the style carries little or no risk, often suggests investing in contrary, disliked market segments.

This book is divided into three parts. Part I is composed of Chapters 1–3. The first chapter initially focuses on the definition and identification of market segments, and reviews the major equity market segments that concern institutional investors today. Chapter 2 describes the equity market in economic terms and uses simple supply/demand relationships to set a foundation for anticipating and analyzing the performance associated with various style investment strategies. Part I concludes with Chapter 3, which describes how investor expectations influence the resulting transaction prices within that supply and demand economic market framework.

Part II, Chapters 4–8, reviews the major market segments and style investment strategies that are of concern to institutional investors today. The five chapters review the various segments but, more importantly, each chapter analyzes the historical performance of each segment of style strategy within the context of both the economic and expectational framework outlined in Part I.

Part III, Chapters 9–11, attempts to join Parts I and II by discussing issues and problems that are currently being discussed by equity market participants. In particular, the implications for pension plan sponsors are outlined, and the use of equity derivatives is explained.

Contents

1

Understanding and Defining Market Segmentation

Although investors tend to refer to the "market," intuitively most would agree that all stocks do not behave identically. For example, there have been pronounced historical periods when smaller capitalization stocks outperformed larger capitalization stocks, and when value-oriented stocks outperformed growth-oriented stocks. Similarly, there have been periods when consumer-oriented stocks perform well, and periods when industrial stocks outperform.

The efficient market theory, developed in the 1950s and 1960s based on the work of Markowitz (1952 and 1959) and Sharpe (1964 and 1970), would suggest that all available information is quickly incorporated into the price of a stock, and that it may be fruitless to attempt to pick individual stocks in an attempt to outperform the overall market. The performance of a stock would ultimately be solely a function of a stock's risk, and returns should increase as the risk of an investment increases in order to compensate the buyer of riskier assets for accepting additional risk. Corollaries of the theory suggest that a stock's or money manager's outperformance over a given period of time might be purely because of chance.

During the 1970s and 1980s, however, academic research began to discuss whether returns within the equity market were indeed consistent with the efficient market hypothesis, or whether the market was segmented. It appeared that the efficient market hypothesis could not account for the outperformance of certain sets of stocks with similar characteristics. If one adjusted the returns of certain groups of stocks to account for the stocks' risk, there remained an unexplained *excess return*. Those segments of excess returns within the equity market should not have occurred if the market were truly efficient.

As a result of the unexplained returns associated with various market segments, academic portfolio research has been fraught with the idea that the original models that attempted to explain the efficient market hypothesis and predict stock returns had been misspecified or were overly simple. Sharpe's original market model of risk suggested that the return of a stock was linearly related to the stock's relative volatility versus that of the overall market (beta). If a stock's volatility within a well-diversified portfolio was twice that of the equity market, then the stock's returns should be roughly twice that of the market. If the market was up 10 percent, then the implied stock return would be 20 percent. If the market goes down 10 percent, then the implied stock return would be -20 percent. Criticisms of that model have centered on whether the sole factor affecting stock performance is the market, and whether the risk/ return relationships within the equity market are indeed linear.

The work of Roll and Ross (1980) is probably among the best-known criticism of the original market model. Roll and Ross's Arbitrage Pricing Theory suggested that the market was probably efficient, but that there were a series of factors that could explain risk better than a single factor alone, namely the "market." Arbitrage pricing theory tends to view stock returns as a function of macroeconomic factors such as the slope of the yield curve, interest rates, industrial production, oil prices, and so on.

The focus of this book is to better identify and understand the performance of equity market segments and styles regardless of whether they are merely the result of a misspecified model. The fact remains that practitioners have managed money successfully for some time by adhering to the unexplained market anomalies associated with the original market model. The investment world appears to have come to grips with market segmentation and developed investment products to exploit such anomalies long before the academic world was willing to agree that such efficient market anomalies even existed.

In reality, there may be structural, psychological, or informational asymmetries among market participants which may make the simultaneous digestion of investment information by all parties impossible. Those asymmetries, no matter how irrational, may be the reason that market anomalies exist. In addition, there may be a philosophical problem that we will discuss later as to whether the market can discount future events with complete certainty.

A simple definition, therefore, of equity market segments might be groups of stocks with similar characteristics that tend to perform as a group over several economic and market cycles. Anomalies are market segments that cannot be explained by traditional risk models. Style investing is that done in an attempt to exploit market anomalies. All anomalies are in themselves market segments, but not all segments are necessarily accepted market anomalies.

Although certainly not new at the time, *style investing* began to spread rapidly within the institutional investor community during the 1980s, and the proliferation of style-oriented managers can probably be attributed to the advent of the pension consultant. Consultants are usually hired by pension plan sponsors to act as a sort of consumer advocate. The consultant helps the plan sponsor search for managers who might fit the plan's goals, monitors manager performance, and makes suggestions to the plan sponsor regarding potential manager changes either because of poor performance or because of the changing goals of the plan. Consultants tend to partition managers according to the market anomalies and styles that the managers follow in order to find managers who are good at a specific task. The consultant attempts to make sure that the manager is a "good" manager, and also whether he or she is successful within the particular style. Consultants usually do not favor managers who switch styles because, without a set style discipline, it becomes more difficult to understand whether a manager truly has skill or whether a manager is simply lucky. In addition, it is easier to set goals for the pension plan with managers who are focused. If most managers are style focused, and the customer (namely, the plan sponsor) finds that to be preferable, then the manager who is not style focused is placed at a marketing disadvantage. Thus, most money managers are now style focused.

There are few institutional equity managers who do not classify themselves as using some style of equity management. The terms *growth* and *value*, for example, although first written about perhaps more than forty years ago, have become central terms within the institutional investor vernacular during the 1980s because of the events described previously.

Most style investing is microeconomically based, meaning that equity managers tend to pay more attention to the underlying characteristics of specific companies than to the macroeconomy. Much of this book, however, is based on the notion that style investing and the macroeconomy are directly linked, and that equity managers may make grave mistakes when separating the two.

◆ Better-Known Market Segments

Market segments can probably be separated into two groups, namely macroeconomic and microeconomic, but practitioners often refer to segments as being *top-down* or *bottom-up*. Top-down analysis is that which begins with the macroeconomy (the top) and works its way down until one examines individual companies. Top-down analysis might be more concerned with how industrial production affects machinery companies, than with the relative valuation of company A versus company B. Bottom-up analysis, however, begins with individual company data (the bottom) and works upward to form a portfolio. Top-down segments are usually defined in terms of the overall macroeconomy, while bottom-up segments are usually based on the characteristics of individual firms. An example of a top-down segment might be *cyclical* stocks, while an example of a bottom-up one might be *highly leveraged* stocks.

Most investors are generally aware of top-down market segments because market observers often comment on economic sector and industry groups. Using our definition of market segments, one would be defining potential market segments when one describes

Financial stocks or Consumer Staples, or even when one defines an industry group. Standard & Poor's defines more than ninety industry groups within its publications and, for all practical purposes, it has potentially defined more than ninety separate market segments.[1]

Table 1.1 highlights various top-down segments. Most should be familiar because, as mentioned, they are discussed regularly without thought to market segmentation. Top-down market segments are generally thought to be influenced by the overall macroeconomy. For example, cyclical sectors, such as Basic Industrials or Capital Goods, would tend to outperform the overall equity market when the economy is expanding. On the other hand, more stable categories, such as Consumer Staples, would tend to outperform as the economy weakens.

Figure 1.1 demonstrates that top-down segments do indeed perform quite differently through time by comparing the performance of the Standard & Poor's Consumer Goods Index with the S&P Capital Goods Index. As the line rises in the chart, the Capital Goods Index is outperforming, but the Consumer Goods Index is outperforming as the line falls. One can see that during the 1980s, companies with significant exposure to the industrial economy significantly underperformed, while companies with little or no ex-

Table 1.1   Top-Down Market Segments

Sectors	Industries
Credit Cyclicals	Homebuilders, S&Ls
Consumer Growth Staples	Drugs, Soft Drinks
Consumer Cyclicals	Autos, Appliances
Consumer Staples	Foods, Household Products
Capital Goods	Machinery, Electrical Equip.
Technology	Computer Systems, Telecom.
Energy	Oils, Coal
Basic Industrials	Chemicals, Aluminums
Financials	Banks, Insurance Cos.
Transportation	Airlines, Railroads
Utilities	Electric, Natural Gas
Conglomerates	

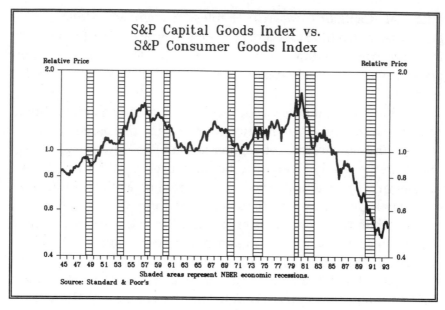

Figure 1.1   Capital vs. Consumer Goods Relative Performance

posure tended to outperform. Table 1.2 further points out the disparate performance of the constituents of these indices during the 1970s and 1980s. For comparison, Table 1.3 lists bottom-up market segments. An example of a bottom-up market segment with which most investors are probably quite familiar are stock divisions by size and the so-called "small stock effect." Usually, market segments by size are determined by stocks' market values (current stock price times shares outstanding), but such separations can be made by size of total assets, size of sales, and so on. Most institutional investors, however, define size according to market capitalization because of the trading liquidity problems that small companies often present. A company that might have large total sales figures may have a small market capitalization within the equity market perhaps because its sales, while still absolutely large, may be declining through time. Thus, it might be impossible for an institutional investor to take a position in that stock simply because not enough of the stock regularly trades or because, if one invested only a small proportion of a portfolio in the company, then one

Table 1.2   **Capital Goods vs. Consumer Goods Constituent Performance**

	Median	*Average*	*Highest*	*Lowest*
1971–79				
Cap. Goods	2.7%	86.8%	608.2%	−16.4%
Con. Goods	−8.8%	18.1%	277.5%	−57.8%
1980–92				
Cap. Goods	92.5%	228.8%	1117.3%	−18.2%
Con. Goods	703.1%	764.8%	1511.9%	147.3%

Table 1.3   **Bottom-Up Market Segments**

Category	*Potential Measurement*
Size	Market Value, Sales, Assets
Risk	Beta, Debt/Equity Ratios
Valuation	P/E, P/B, P/CF
Growth Characteristics	High Growth, Stable Growth

would end up owning a sizable portion of the equity of the company beyond what might be considered prudent.

Perhaps the best-known studies of the "small stock effect" are those by Ibbotson and Sinquefield (1976) and Banz (1981). They initially pointed out that smaller capitalization stocks significantly outperformed larger ones over a multidecade time period. Those studies demonstrated that the results held even if one accounted for the additional volatility (risk) that accompanied those higher returns. In other words, the risk-adjusted returns of smaller capitalization stocks could not be explained by the efficient market hypothesis.

Figure 1.2 shows the relative performance of small stocks versus large stocks beginning in 1926. It is again a relative performance chart, so as the line rises it indicates that small stocks were outperforming. When the line falls in the chart, it indicates that larger stocks outperformed. One can see that although there are distinct periods when smaller capitalization stocks outperform or underperform larger ones, the overall slope of the line suggests that small stock returns over the entire period were far superior to those of large stocks.

Table 1.4 shows that performance to be superior even if one were to account for the risk of smaller capitalization stocks. The first column shows the average annual returns for both smaller stocks and for the S&P 500 from 1926 to 1992. The second column displays the beta (or risk measured in terms of volatility relative to the S&P 500) of the returns of the Ibbotson Small Stock Index used in Figure 1.2. The third column shows the implied return according to Sharpe's simple market model.[2] The fourth column shows the excess return above the return suggested by the market model. The beta of smaller capitalization stocks is indeed higher

Table 1.4   Excess Returns of Small Stocks

Avg. Annual Return	Beta	Implied Return	"Excess" Return
S&P500: 12.4%	1.00	12.4%	0.0%
Small: 17.8%	1.38	17.1%	0.7%

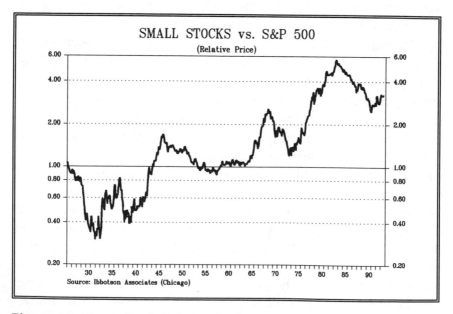

Figure 1.2   Small Stock Relative Performance Chart

than that for their larger counterparts (the S&P 500 has a beta of 1.00 by definition), and the efficient market theory suggests that the returns should be purely a function of that increased beta-related risk. However, small stock returns are greater than their beta times the market return and, therefore, have an unexplained excess return. In fact, smaller stocks appear to have about a 70 basis point annual excess return.

In Chapter 8, we will attempt to examine some of the factors that influence the relative performance of small and large stocks, and why the cycles appear in the long-term performance figure.

As mentioned before regarding money managers who oversee pension money, a recent accelerating trend among mutual funds is to define one's fund as either a growth or value fund. The increased use of such delineations demonstrates that the relationship between firm specific microeconomics and stock performance is becoming more widely known, although perhaps no better understood.

Defining *growth* and *value*, per se, is actually quite difficult. A very simple definition (more complex definitions will follow in later chapters) might be that stocks carrying a growth connotation are those that have displayed earnings growth superior to that of the overall market, while value stocks are those that have shown inferior or highly variable growth that investors find generally unappealing.

As we will see later, the historical performance of these two investment styles appears to be highly dependent on the overall level of earnings growth within the economy, and that will be the main topic of several later chapters. Figure 1.3 demonstrates the relative total return performance of an index of nine growth mutual funds versus nine value mutual funds. As the line rises, growth funds historically outperformed value funds, but the opposite was true when the line falls. Note that there appear to be both secular, long-term performance trends as well as shorter-term cycles of relative performance.

◆ Lesser-Known Market Segments

Bottom-up segments, unlike the ones already discussed, tend to be somewhat more difficult to understand and, thus, most bottom-

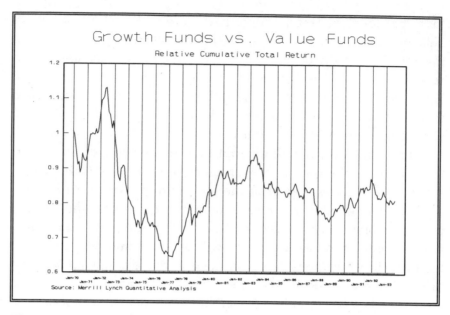

Figure 1.3 Growth vs. Value Funds

up market segments are generally not discussed either among institutional investors or within the popular press. Whereas one can generally understand that fewer cars will be bought as unemployment rises, it is more difficult to understand why highly leveraged companies tend to outperform during periods of inflation.

Often investors look for "good" companies and expect them to be "good" stocks; however, history suggests that this is not always the case. Solt and Statman (1989) pointed out, "good" companies often end up being "bad" stocks. More recent work (see Bernstein and Pradhuman, 1993) has shown that market segments actually exist relating to the quality of a company. There are indeed periods when "good" companies make "good" stocks, but then there are also times when "bad" companies make "good" stocks. Figure 1.4 demonstrates the relative performance of "good" and "bad" companies by comparing an index comprised of stocks rated C and D by Standard & Poor's versus an index comprised of stocks rated A+. Once again, the figure demonstrates relative performance, so the C and D stocks outperformed as the line rises. There have been distinct periods when one would have wanted to be a

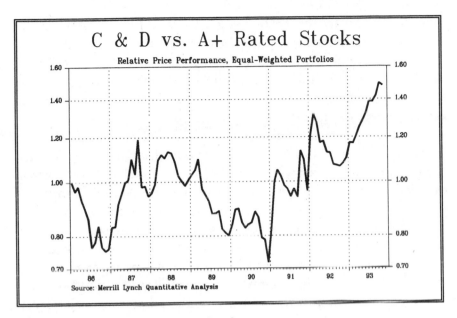

Figure 1.4 A+ vs. C/D Rate Stocks

high-quality investor and periods when one would have wanted to be a low-quality investor.

Chapter 5 is dedicated to understanding why there have historically been periods during which low-quality companies outperform, and through periods during which there is a high-quality bias to performance. Contrary to what one might think, "good" companies seem to often make "bad" stocks over the longer term.

Investors are often concerned about the risk of an investment, and the market tends to form segments according to the risk characteristics of stocks. Definitions and measurements of risk will be discussed later, however, the previously mentioned beta statistic attempts to measure the risk of a stock within the context of a well-diversified portfolio. The efficient market theorists felt that the risks solely associated with a particular stock, such as the chairman's death, would be canceled out when stocks were held in a well-diversified portfolio. Thus, the only risk investors need concern themselves with was the risk that could not be diversified away and was related solely to the risk of the overall market. As we mentioned earlier, the theory suggests that higher beta, riskier stocks should outperform lower beta, safer stocks through time.

High beta and low beta stocks have indeed performed quite differently through time. We will examine what affects the performance of market segments delineated by beta, and whether beta is indeed dead, as many studies purported over the past few years.

There are several chapters in this book that examine market segments delineated according to various risk measures. In fact, the notion of high- versus low-quality could itself be a comparison of risk characteristics because investors *perceive* "good" companies to have few risks and "bad" companies to have many.

One of the newer and more interesting measures of risk among equities has been borrowed from the fixed-income market. The term *duration* has been used for some time among fixed-income investors to refer to the interest rate sensitivity of a bond or note. The greater the interest rate sensitivity, the greater the volatility of the returns of the bond and, therefore, the greater the risk to the holder. More recently, duration risk has been applied to equities. The market does appear to segment stocks according to interest rate sensitivity, and we will see in Chapter 8 that there appears to actually be a yield curve within the equity market, similar to those commonly discussed regarding the fixed-income market.

This book will only examine what I consider to be major market segments and style considerations within the equity market today. That does not say that there are no others, nor does it say that these particular segments will remain intact. The market most likely goes through an evolutionary process, and within a surprisingly short period of time the market segments found today will likely be joined or replaced by others that have so far gone unnoticed.

◈ *Summary*

♦ Although investors often refer to the "market," most would agree that all stocks do not perform similarly.

♦ The efficient market theorists believed that the market quickly digested all available investment information, and that stock returns were uniform and linearly proportional to risk.

♦ Academics found, however, that the models that tried to predict returns based on the risk of a stock could not account for the outperformance of certain groups of stocks. The uncovered anomalies to the efficient market theory suggested that the equity market did not behave as one market, but rather was segmented.

♦ Market segments are groups of stocks with similar characteristics that tend to perform similarly. All market anomalies are segments, but not all segments are necessarily market anomalies.

♦ Market segments can be divided into top-down and bottom-up classifications.

♦ Although that division can be made, the macroeconomy and a firm's microeconomics are interrelated.

This book will attempt to focus on those interrelationships as a source for understanding the performance of market segments and investment styles.

♦ Notes

1. For example, see "Stocks in the S&P 500," published monthly by Standard & Poor's Corporation.
2. The formula for the market model is as follows:

$$\text{Stock Return} = \alpha + \beta(\text{Market Return}) + e,$$

where,

α = "alpha," or the mispricing of the stock,
β = "beta," or a risk measure within the context of a well-diversified portfolio,
e = random error term.

We have included only beta in the table within the text, although the model incorporates and alpha and error term. The efficient market theory suggests that alphas should generally be zero for an overall portfolio of stocks.

◆ References

Banz, Rolf W., "The Relationship Between Return and Market Value of Common Stocks," *Journal of Financial Economics*, 1981, vol. 9, no. 1, pp. 3–18.

Bernstein, Richard and Pradhuman, Satya, "Introducing the MLQA Quality Indices," *Merrill Lynch Quantitative Viewpoint*, March 23, 1993.

Ibbotson, Roger G. and Sinquefield, Rex A., "Stocks, Bonds, Bills, and Inflation: Year-by-Year Historical Returns (1926–1974)," *Journal of Business*. 1976, vol. 49, no. 1, pp. 11–47.

Markowitz, Harry M., "Portfolio Selection," *Journal of Finance*, 1952, vol. 7, no. 1, pp. 77–91.

Markowitz, Harry M., *Portfolio Selection: Efficient Diversification of Investments* (New Haven: Yale University Press, 1959).

Roll, Richard and Ross, Stephen A., "An Empirical Investigation of the Arbitrage Pricing Theory," *Journal of Finance*, 1980, vol. 35, no. 5, pp. 1073–1103.

Sharpe, William F., "Capital Asset Prices: A Theory of Market Equilibrium Under Conditions of Risk," *Journal of Finance*, 1964, vol. 19, no. 3, pp. 425–442.

Sharpe, William F., *Portfolio Theory and Capital Markets* (New York: McGraw-Hill Book Company, 1970).

Solt, Michael and Statman, Meir, "Good Companies, Bad Stocks," *Journal of Portfolio Management*, 1989, vol. 15, no. 4, pp. 39–44.

2

The Economics of Nominal Earnings Growth and Investor Risk Perception

*T*he economist plays a major role within Wall Street research. Fundamental analysts incorporate into their recommendations forecasts of the economy for inflation, industrial production, consumer purchases, and building activity, to name a few, in order to estimate sales and earnings trends for companies. Portfolio managers use economic forecasts to make judgments about asset allocation, style, sector, and segment rotation. In addition, both groups use economists' profits forecasts to help them gauge relative valuation and relative earnings growth.

Perhaps the most important piece of information within an economic forecast for a style investor may be whether corporate profitability is expected to rise or fall within the economy because it appears as though the overriding factor influencing the performance of market segments is the abundance or scarcity of earnings growth (see Bernstein, 1990). It sometimes appears, however, as though style-oriented investors burden themselves with extraneous economic information. Today's Wall Street economic forecasts are full of details regarding production, profitability, income, investment, consumption, and exports. Although these are all important assessments regarding the contours of future economic growth, the style-oriented investor should primarily worry about whether the overall corporate sector is profitable, and whether that profitability will increase or decrease.

Transaction prices within the equity market, like those within any economic market, reflect buyers' views regarding the value of a good worth purchasing relative to those of sellers. If the particular good being sold is scarce or takes a great deal of skill to manufacture, then buyers might be willing to pay a higher price for the product than they would if the good were common. However, if a particular good is abundant or easy to produce, then buyers would probably be unwilling to pay a high price for the product. For example, we pay a higher price for diamonds than we do for apples because diamonds are scarcer. If diamonds grew on trees and we could plant those trees ourselves, then one could rest assured that diamonds would be considerably cheaper than they are today.

The product bought and sold within the equity market is profits growth. Equities represent partial ownership in a company and shareholders have claims to the profits and assets of the corporation of which they own stock. Investors buy shares to be partial owners in a company that they feel will grow its profits and increase the value of the corporation's assets which will, in turn, increase the value of ownership and increase the stock price. They hope that they will reap a higher return by owning stock in a particular company than that provided by other investments. Stock price performance and return on investment are, therefore, determined by the corporation's ability to grow its profits. Companies that can grow profits at a superior rate tend to have stocks that outperform the overall stock market, and those that cannot tend to have underperforming stocks.

If superior profits growth became scarce, one would think that investors would be willing to pay higher prices to obtain ownership in the companies that can indeed produce superior growth. Conversely, if earnings growth was abundant, investors might be foolish to pay high prices for an abundant resource. In other words, there are periods during which investors treat earnings growth like diamonds because earnings growth is perceived to be so scarce, and there are times when they treat it like apples because it appears so abundant.

16

The equity market is denominated in nominal terms, yet economists generally discuss their forecast in real terms. Real figures are those that are not affected by inflation and, therefore, better reflect the number of units of a good that are being produced. Real growth is extremely important because it measures the actual unit output of an economy. Increased output, not rising prices, leads to sustainable, long-term job creation and a higher standard of living within an economy. Unit growth is obviously also important for a company, but such analyses ignore any potential pricing flexibility that a company might have. It is naive to think that a company that is producing units at an increasing rate might not be tempted to raise prices as well. Thus, the equity market is a nominal market, and it is nominal, not real, earnings growth that influences stock prices. In other words, inflation helps the stocks of those companies whose product prices are inflating.

Figure 2.1 shows the year-to-year percent change of the Standard & Poor's Drug Index plotted against the year-to-year percent change in the Consumer Price Index for Prescription Drugs; Figure 2.2 shows the year-to-year percent change in the S&P Steel Index

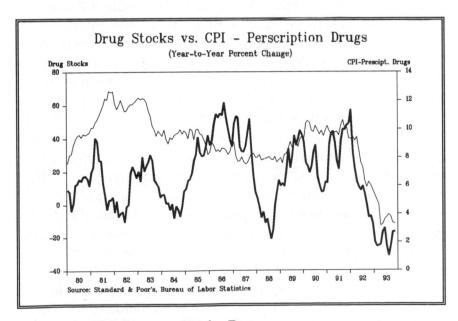

Figure 2.1 S&P Drug vs. CPI for Drugs

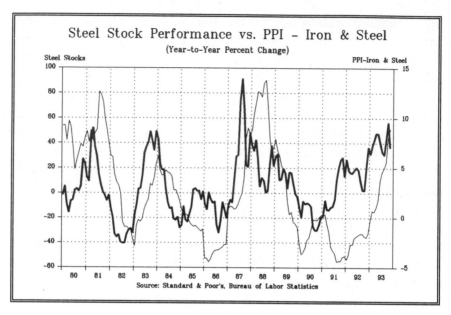

Figure 2.2   S&P Steel vs. PPI for Steel

against the year-to-year percent change in the Producer Price Index for steel. The figures are good examples that when prices rise for a specific good, the stock prices of the companies that manufactured that good also generally rise. On the other hand, stock price performance erodes when prices grow less quickly or decline. Sometimes, prices for a particular good rise because of its proprietary nature and significant product demand, but other times they decline because the particular product has become more of a commodity of which there is overwhelming supply. A newer company with new products will tend to experience the first situation, while a more mature company might face the latter.

The relationship between product pricing flexibility and stock performance often causes investors and corporate managers to view companies as growth companies when, in fact, they are merely the beneficiaries of inflation. As the figures show, both steel and drug companies experienced such periods historically despite our current perceptions of both groups. The rise in prescription prices during the 1980s led investors to consider the drug group a growth category, while steels are now considered the epitome of a mature industry.

Nominal earnings growth can be affected by things other than inflation and unit growth. For example, increased productivity, or the output of a company per labor hour or per machine can greatly enhance profitability. A company may modernize a plant in order to produce twice the number of units in the same time it might have taken in its older plant. Or, the firm may not want to produce more units, but rather produce them in half the time it previously took. Thus, as companies become more productive, nominal earnings growth will generally become more abundant because more goods are being produced, not because prices are being raised. Economists often stress the importance of productivity within a competitive global economy because productivity allows increased and sustainable nominal profitability and nominal growth without inflation.

The abundance or scarcity of nominal earnings growth will affect how market segments and investing styles perform. When growth is scarce, the equity market will bid up the prices of those stocks that can maintain or increase their earnings growth rates during that tough period. However, when growth is abundant and a larger number of companies are growing, equity market participants will comparison shop among growing companies, and different segments and styles will perform better than those that would if growth were scarce. Market segments and styles perform differently depending on the availability of the equity market's product, namely nominal profits growth.

A simple way to measure the abundance or scarcity of nominal earnings growth is simply to look at reported earnings momentum for the Standard & Poor's 500 Index. I define earnings momentum as the latest four quarters of reported earnings divided by those from a year ago. Figure 2.3 shows S&P 500 earnings momentum from the late 1940s. When the bars are above 0, that implies that earnings momentum is positive, and that a larger number of companies are probably growing their earnings. When the bars are below 0, it implies that earnings momentum is negative, and that profits growth is relatively more scarce. It is interesting to note that

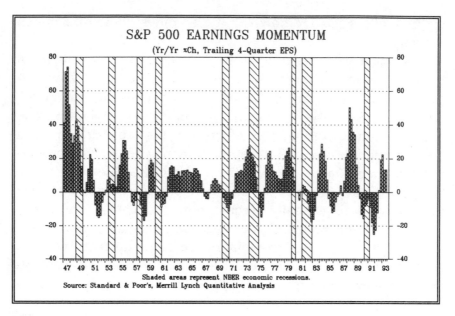

Figure 2.3 S&P 500 EPS Momentum from 1945

the late 1980s to early 1990s were the longest profits "recession" in the entire post-war period, which might help to explain the explosive popularity during that period of investment strategies based on the scarcity of growth.

Earnings momentum, as we have defined it, demonstrates whether nominal earnings growth is available, but the market will tend to anticipate the abundance or scarcity of growth and will react to changes in the amount of overall nominal earnings growth *on the margin*, or in terms of the differences in the height of the bars in the figure. Figure 2.3 therefore, becomes more helpful if one assumes that profits growth is becoming increasingly abundant from the trough to the peak of the bars (or perhaps as the bars go from −10 percent to +10 percent). Similarly, growth would be increasingly scarce as the bars move from peak to trough (from +10 percent to −10 percent).

Using terms from calculus, the first derivative of earnings momentum (or the second derivative of earnings) appears to influence the relative performance of different investment styles. As we will see in more detail later, when the first derivative of earnings momentum is positive (the bars are getting taller), the equity market will tend to reward those companies that will be the catalysts for the increased level of growth, and penalize companies that maintain their growth rates or have declining rates of growth. When the first derivative of earnings momentum is negative (the bars are getting shorter), the market will tend to reward those companies that maintain their growth, while it penalizes those that have declining growth rates.

The rate of growth in earnings can be affected by a number of factors other than the economy. Obviously, the overall economy, inflation, and productivity play perhaps the largest roles in determining the level of corporate profitability. Further, accounting rules may also alter the level of reported earnings. United States companies, and foreign companies that want to list their stocks on American stock exchanges, must adhere to what is usually referred to as Generally Accepted Accounting Principles (GAAP). In addition, the Financial Accounting Standards Board (FASB) determines what financial information must be reported to the investing public, and how that information must be presented. Sometimes when FASB rules change, earnings may be temporarily affected, either positively or negatively. It remains unclear as to whether temporary changes in earnings caused by accounting rules changes materially impact stock returns. Throughout this book, however, we will assume that accounting changes have no material impact on stock prices.

Several times during the previous paragraphs, we have referred to *reported* earnings, and that distinction is made because the term *operating earnings* has become popular within the Wall Street vernacular. The term refers to earnings that are higher up on the income statement than reported earnings, and generally exclude one-time charges to earnings that a company might take. Management may have many different motives for taking a write-off, including a poor economy, an underperforming business segment, corporate reorganization costs, and management compensation plans that are structured in such a way so that management might benefit from a reduced book value of the company in future years are only a few (Bernstein and Pradhuman, 1992).

A writeoff refers to the action a company takes when the value of a particular asset that the company owns falls below the asset's historical carrying value on the balance sheet, and the company's management decides that the asset is no longer a productive part of the overall corporate assets. The historical value of an asset is commonly called its *book value*, and GAAP accounting, which always attempts to err on the side of conservatism, states that assets such as plant and equipment must be listed on the balance sheet at that historical purchase value less depreciation. Writeoffs occur when the corporation realizes that the asset is worth less than what the book value would imply. Rather than continuing to slowly depreciate an unproductive asset and possibly lose money on the operation of an obsolete asset, the company will write the asset off its balance sheet all at once.

Accounting journal entries must balance. For every credit there must be an equal debit. For every asset there must be an equal liability. Therefore, a firms' total assets must equal its liabilities plus net worth. One cannot create assets without adding liabilities or increasing net worth. Conversely, if the asset base of a company is shrinking, then the corporation must decrease its liabilities or decrease net worth. In many cases, liabilities are fixed (such as long-term debt outstanding), and therefore, writing off an asset would not reduce liabilities. Thus, writeoffs generally reduce net worth.

When companies write down assets, they must take one-time charges against earnings in order to reduce net worth. The writeoff does not require the company to pay anyone from earnings, but assets and liabilities would not match if the company added the current period's earnings to existing retained earnings. Thus, to reduce retained earnings by the amount of the written-off asset, a corporation must reduce the current earnings contribution to net worth by the amount of the asset.

If the company were able to sell the asset rather than write it off the books, then a one-time, nonrecurring charge would not be taken, but rather a one-time gain might occur (assuming the company made a profit on the sale). The gain, opposite to the writeoff, would indeed be counted in reported earnings. Thus, whereas writeoffs tend to decrease the availability of earnings growth, one-time gains on sales of assets tend to increase the availability of earnings growth.

During the late 1980s, the combination of declining economic growth and the lack of inflation led corporations to take writeoffs at an historically high rate because asset values actually began to decline or deflate. In other words, when overall nominal growth is strong (often simply because of inflation) even the oldest, most inefficient asset still contributes to a company's production because rising prices will offset the effects that slow production might otherwise have on profitability. Subsequently, during a period of disinflation or outright deflation, those assets quickly become obsolete. Slow production, relative to that of one's competitors, combined with the inability to raise prices generally paves the road to bankruptcy. Therefore, writeoffs increased dramatically during the second half of the 1980s, and reported profits were extremely weak. Figure 2.3 showed that the longest profits recession of the entire post-war period took place during the late 1980s, and writeoffs were a major contributor to that profits recession.

Throughout this book we will concentrate on reported earnings, rather than operating earnings, as the catalyst for cycles of style investing. Again, operating earnings are generally those that come from the continuing operations of the company. Therefore, they exclude writeoffs because the written-off asset will generally not continue to operate. The problem for investors is that operating and reported earnings are nearly identical for some companies, but significantly different for others.

Rational investors should be more willing to buy the company that does not take a writeoff if all other things are equal. For example, assume two companies have the same valuation, the same historical earnings growth, and the same growth prospects for the future. However, the similar statistics for company A are on a reported basis, while those for company B are on an operating, pre-writeoff basis. Company A will be more likely to outperform when earnings growth is scarce because its earnings are true bottom line earnings, while those for company B are not. If earnings were scarce, then the market would probably place a premium on Company A because it is producing true earnings and increasing net worth relative to Company B, which is actually in the process of reducing net worth.

Figure 2.4 demonstrates how much writeoffs have affected reported earnings by showing the annual level of writeoffs for the S&P 500 on a per-share basis. A level of $0.50 suggests that S&P 500 earnings per share were increased by $0.50 per share because of one-time gains during the quarter. A reading of −$0.50 indicates that S&P 500 earnings per share were reduced by $0.50 largely because of writeoffs. One can see that writeoffs have been quite voluminous during the late 1980s and early 1990s.

Table 2.1 highlights the results of a simple regression equation that examined the relationship between stock price performance during 1990 and a stock's projected five-year earnings growth rate according to the I/B/E/S database, valuation as measured by price/book value, and size as measured by market capitalization all at the end of 1989. In addition, we added a "dummy" variable to signify whether a company took a writeoff during 1990. The "dummy" variable has a value of either 0 or 1 depending on

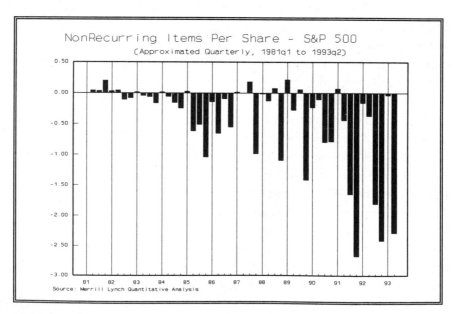

Figure 2.4 The Level of Writeoffs

Table 2.1   Writeoffs' Impact on 1990 Performance

Variable	Coefficient	t-Statistic	Significant?
"Constant"	13.56%		
Market Value	0.00%	1.78	No
Proj. Growth	0.96%	4.35	Yes
Price/Book	−0.02%	−0.23	No
Writeoff?	−15.36%	−4.51	Yes

N = 482, R² = 0.08

whether the particular company took a writeoff during 1990. The variable takes on a value of 1 if the company did have a writeoff, and 0 otherwise. 1990 was chosen as the year to study because the economy was in a recession, and earnings growth was becoming increasingly scarce. Thus, it was a good year to test if the equity market did indeed penalize companies for a lack of reported earnings simply because of writeoffs.

The second column of the summary table shows the marginal effect that a one-unit change in the particular variable had on the average stock's performance during the subsequent year, while the third column shows the variable's *t-statistic*. The t-statistic indicates whether the variable's impact is statistically significant, or whether the relationship is merely attributable to chance. Generally, a t-statistic greater than 1.96 or less than −1.96 suggests that the relationship is significant.

Although not all the variables are significant (for instance, price/book value had a t-statistic of −0.23), the "dummy" variable that indicates whether a company took a writeoff during the year is indeed significant, and the coefficient is quite large. The −15.36 percent suggests that the market penalized those companies that took writeoffs, and that their stock price performance was hurt by more than 15 percent on average solely because of their taking a writeoff.

Of course the "dummy" variable could be capturing the effect of many underlying similarities among companies and could be a gross simplification. Nonetheless, the magnitude and significance of the writeoff "dummy" suggests that equity market participants did look at least somewhat unfavorably upon firms that took write-offs during 1990.

One year may not be a representative sample of how the equity market reacts to writeoffs, therefore, in later chapters we will show that the cycles of style investing do indeed react to the levels of reported earnings momentum.

The abundance or scarcity of reported earnings growth may alter investors' risk perceptions. Investors appear to be generally more willing to take a risk when nominal earnings growth becomes more abundant, and more conservative when earnings growth becomes scarce. Going back to our diamonds and apples analogy, because diamonds are scarce, diamond buyers are conservative. Before buying a high-priced diamond, they will have it appraised to make sure that it is indeed the high-quality diamond that the seller has represented it as. Have you ever known anyone to get an apple appraised? Thus, when growth becomes scarce, investors will become more conservative, and tend to buy "known" growth. They will tend to be more willing to gamble on potential growth when growth becomes more abundant.

What appears strange, however, is that market participants often accept the market's appraisal of "known" growth apparently without question. We will see in Chapter 3 that fears about growth and the acceptance of the market's appraisal of future growth may often lead to underperformance. The simple acceptance of "known" growth (or for that matter "known" dogs) may be very similar to Shiller's comments on investment fads and bubbles (1989). He argues that social and psychological phenomena relating to human behavior disrupt the market's efficient pricing mechanism. Thus, investors will react overenthusiastically toward some stocks and drive their prices well above reasonable value, while other, undervalued stocks go completely ignored.

The equity market obviously differs in one major way from the diamond market that we have used for comparison. The supply of diamonds can change, but not as dramatically or as quickly as the supply of nominal earnings growth. There is often talk of diamond cartels controlling the availability of high-quality diamonds, but earnings growth can change from declining 20 percent to rising 20 percent within a year.

That difference means that investors must always be aware of the amount of nominal earnings growth available, and closely follow the forecasts and changes in the forecasts of such growth. In the next chapter, we will see that when investors finally become universally convinced that earnings growth will remain poor and, as a result, become severely conservative, one should begin to invest using the assumption that earnings growth will improve. In later chapters, we will see how indicators such as the shape of the government bond market yield curve, government/corporate bonds spreads, and the dividend payout ratio can be used to aid in style rotation strategies by gauging when equity investors have become overly cautious or overly aggressive.

◆ Summary

- ◆ The product bought and sold within the equity market is nominal earnings growth.

- ◆ The macroeconomy will affect the supply of nominal earnings growth, but so will accounting changes and one-time charges.

- ◆ The abundance or scarcity of nominal earnings growth will affect how market segments and styles will perform.

- ◆ A simple method for measuring the abundance or scarcity of earnings growth is to look at reported earnings momentum for the S&P 500.

- ◆ Reported earnings are more important than the operating earnings that have become so popular among Wall Street analysts.

- ◆ The abundance or scarcity of nominal earnings growth alters investors' risk perceptions. They generally become more conservative when growth becomes scarce, and more willing to accept risk when growth is abundant.

◆ References

Bernstein, Richard, "Growth & Value—Part III," *Merrill Lynch Quantitative Viewpoint*, October 23, 1990.

Bernstein, Richard, and Pradhuman, Satya D., "Special Report: Writeoffs & Restructuring," *Merrill Lynch Quantitative Viewpoint*, May 19, 1992.

Shiller, Robert J., *Market Volatility* (Cambridge, Massachusetts: The MIT Press, 1989).

3

The Importance of Expectations

*I*f "good" companies do not always make "good" stocks, then why do people tend to invest in "good" companies? If stocks with high projected growth rates tend to underperform the market through time, then why do investors search for stocks with above average projected growth rates? If low price/earnings (P/E) companies outperform the market through time, then why don't investors invest in them? The answers to those questions probably show that *investments are generally made based on perception rather than on reality.*

It is often said that the equity market "discounts" future events. Those who support that contention believe that the equity market assesses the probability of a future event coming true, the outcome of that event, and the investment ramifications long before the event actually occurs. In other words, if one were to wait for an event to occur before investing, then one would probably be too late because the investment implications would already have been priced into the particular investment.

The notion that the equity market "discounts" future events necessarily leads one to the conclusion that the equity market prices stocks based on perception, rather than on reality. Future events that are supposedly being discounted have not yet occurred. Therefore, stock price movements reflect investors' changing perceptions of what will occur, but not what will certainly occur. If the market was able to discount an event with complete certainty, then one could argue that there should be no subsequent price volatility other than that which reflects the time cost of money. For example, if an event was correctly discounted six months before it actually occurred, investors would expect to be paid the six-month rate of interest while they wait for the event. Thus, price volatility should only result from the decay of the time-related interest rate (that is, as it moved from a six-month rate to a five-month rate, and so on) if the market could indeed anticipate with complete certainty.

This argument demonstrates a potential flaw in the efficient market hypothesis. Although the market might actually be quite efficient in pricing investor expectations, market participants cannot do so with complete certainty. Any valuation that the market places on a future event and its outcome might be constantly changing as investors attempt to grasp the ultimate and certain outcome. Thus, the equity market may be an efficient discounter of the current view of future events but, because future events cannot be predicted with complete certainty, the idea of a completely efficient market might actually be impossible.

If the market is good at discounting current perceptions even though those perceptions might change at any moment, then that casts doubt on the value of investment research that attempts to gauge what is coincidentally happening within the economy or what is coincidentally happening to a particular company, because those current perceptions of future events are probably already incorporated into stock prices. Consensus information, in and of itself, has limited investment value because if the data are indeed a reflection of consensus thought and the data are readily available, then the odds are that information is already reflected in stock prices.

The real value of investment research is in discovering how a particular investment view differs from that of the consensus, whether the consensus will move toward that particular view of future events, and the impact that alteration of consensus expectations might have on a stock's price. It is not important whether the economy is growing at 3 percent or that a company is going to earn $1.00 for the quarter. The important information is whether the consensus already accepts those forecasts, what is the probability that the consensus will be wrong, and by how much will the consensus be in error. Because no one can be certain about the future, it therefore becomes more important to gauge the direction of changes in investor perceptions, than to form absolute forecasts.

The difficulty of assessing future events with certainty makes forecasting "earnings surprises" perhaps the most valuable element of fundamental equity research. Earnings surprises can be thought of as situations in which the consensus expected a company to earn $1.00, and it ended up earning $2.00; or vice versa, the consensus expected $2.00, and the company earned only $1.00. Insightful fundamental analysts often highlight the differences between their expectations and those of their counterparts in an attempt to forecast earnings surprises.

Elton, Gruber, and Gultekin (1991) have shown that investors can get excess, risk-adjusted returns if they can forecast how investors will change their perceptions of a company. In other words, if one can forecast earnings surprises, rather than react along with everyone else, one's chances of outperforming the overall market may increase substantially. Their work implies that knowledge of or the ability to forecast *actual* earnings are of little importance to the investment process relative to predicting changes in investor expectations.

It would be added value to the investor if one could predict the probability of when positive or negative earnings surprises are more likely to occur. My general rule of thumb is that when there is little disagreement regarding the outcome of investing in a stock, whether that outcome be positive or negative, then the probability of an earnings surprise increases.

Figure 3.1 highlights what I have called the Earnings Expectations Life Cycle (Bernstein, 1993). It defines the various stages of the evolution of investors' expectations. The expectations for all stocks probably pass through such cycles, although those for individual stocks may not pass through every point on the cycle, and expectations may go around the cycle at different speeds. In addition, stocks may go through minicycles in which they repeat portions of the larger cycle before passing to the next stage.

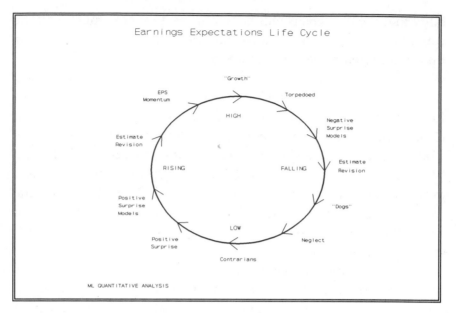

Figure 3.1 Earnings Expectations Life Cycle

The various points on the Earnings Expectations Life Cycle are defined by the many articles written by financial researchers who have studied various aspects of earnings expectations. The Life Cycle may be the first theory that combines that largely disperse research on earnings expectations. The various stages are defined as follows, with references made to specific articles in the Notes at the end of this chapter:

Contrarians: Investors commonly known as contrarians invest in stocks with low earnings expectations. Most investors find these stocks unattractive or overly risky.[1]

Positive Earnings Surprises: Eventually a low-expectations company begins to disseminate more optimistic information; the stock regains investor attention. Research of such stocks may begin to increase.

Positive Earnings Surprise Models: Stock-picking models that search for significant variations between analysts' earnings expectations and actual reported earnings highlight stocks that enjoy positive earnings surprises. Traditional earnings surprise models wait for actual earnings to be reported, hence the models reside in Stage 3 while the event itself may be Stage 2. There has been much written on the earnings surprise effect and stocks' performance.[2]

Estimate Revisions: The consensus begins to raise earnings estimates in response to rising earnings expectations following an earnings surprise. Some analysts' revisions may lag the initial surprise significantly because these analysts may be reluctant to believe that the surprise is a sign of fundamental improvement.

Earnings Momentum: Investors who follow earnings momentum themes begin to buy the stock as estimates and reported earnings continue to rise, and as year-to-year earnings comparisons begin to improve.

"Growth": When strong earnings momentum continues for a long enough period, a stock is termed a "growth" stock by the consensus. These stocks are neither newly identified growth stocks, which are probably uncovered by superior growth-stock investors during Stages 4 and 5, nor are they true growth companies, which alter the business environment.[3] Rather, most investors agree that these stocks are indisputably superior. Earnings expectations for the stocks are very high, hence this is the point on the cycle where there is the maximum risk of disappointment.[4] Contrarian selling would optimally occur at this point on the cycle.

Torpedoed: An earnings disappointment occurs. The stock is torpedoed. Its earnings expectations and price sink.[5]

Negative Earnings Surprise Models: The same models from Stage 3 begin to highlight stocks with lower-than-expected earnings as potential sell candidates.

Estimate Revisions: The consensus begins to lower earnings estimates in response to the earnings disappointment. Again, some analysts tend to lag because they do not believe the earnings shortfall is a sign of a fundamental problem with the company.

"Dogs": After disappointing for a long enough period, these stocks are shunned by investors. Rumors regarding takeover, restructuring, or bankruptcy may affect the stock price temporarily, but investors generally avoid these stocks.

Neglect: Investors have become so disinterested in the stocks or group that brokerage firms begin to believe that research coverage of the group may not be profitable, hence coverage begins to dissipate. The lack of available research information may set the stage for a renewed cycle.[6]

In Chapter 2, I mentioned that investors will tend to search for the "diamonds" of the equity market when growth is scarce, and will tend to search for the "apples" when growth is abundant. The diamonds are often referred to as "growth" stocks, while the "apples" are often referred to as "value" stocks. Growth stocks are ones that have visible earnings growth, while value stocks are those that are bargains relative to the rest of the equity market because investors become overly fearful that the company will fail to grow into the future. (We will discuss growth- and value-oriented investing in considerably more detail in Chapter 4.)

When investors buy growth stocks, they expect to get a "diamond." In other words, they have high expectations for the stocks they are buying, much like the high expectations one has when one purchases a diamond. Thus, growth stock investors probably reside in the top half of the Earnings Expectations Life Cycle (Figure 3.2).

On the other hand, value investors are those who have low expectations for the stocks they are buying. Although one might have certain expectations regarding the apple one buys, it is not a major tragedy, although perhaps shocking, if the apple has a worm. Value investors do not come to the market with high expectations for their stocks. Thus, value investors are generally found in the bottom half of the Life Cycle (Figure 3.3).

Successful investors, however, will always be looking for stocks with rising expectations, regardless of whether the market's

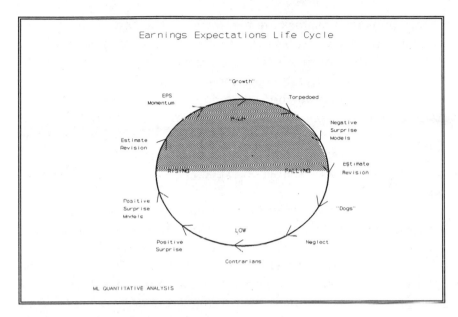

Figure 3.2 Growth Managers

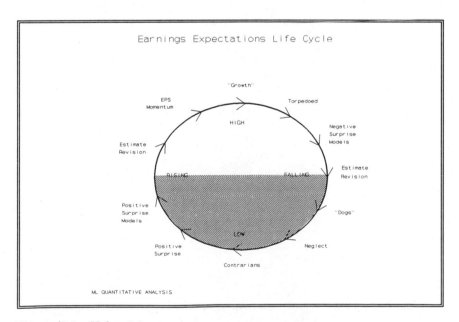

Figure 3.3 Value Managers

expectations for the stock are high or low. The "good" investment manager, therefore, buys stocks that sit on the left side of the life cycle, or the half during which expectations are rising (Figure 3.4).

Unsuccessful investors are those who tend to "buy high, sell low" as a converse to the old saying might go. In terms of the Earnings Expectations Life Cycle, those investors would reside on the right side of the cycle, or the period of falling expectations (Figure 3.5). They buy when expectations are at their most optimistic level, and they sell when expectations are already extremely pessimistic.

If one were to overlay the four half cycles that were just described, one would get the four-slice pie shown in Figure 3.6 that segments the cycle into Good Value, Good Growth, Bad Growth, and Bad Value. The schematic is drawn as a circle because investors tend to incorrectly view the trend for a company's prospects as moving in a straight line. When things are going well for a company, investors will tend to view the trend for a company's potential as a straight line upward, and they will view a company's trend potential as a straight line downward when things are going

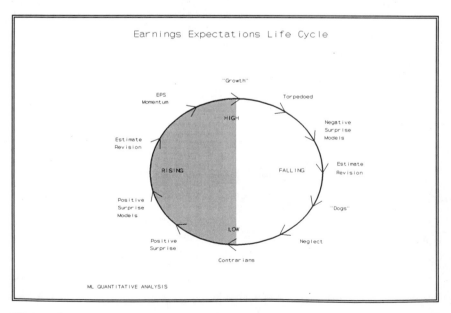

Figure 3.4 "Good" Managers

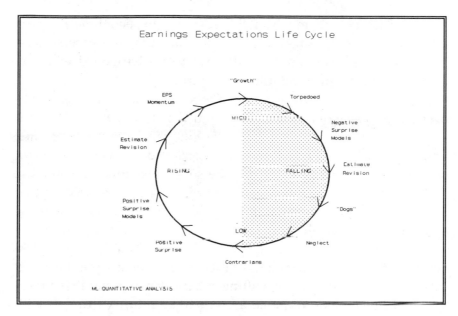

Figure 3.5 "Bad" Managers

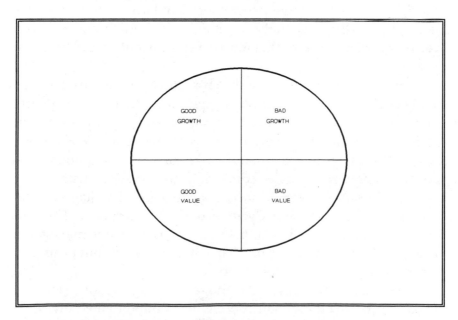

Figure 3.6 Good/Bad/Growth/Value

poorly. History and much of the earnings expectations research cited in this chapter suggest, however, that company prospects do indeed change, and to assume that what has happened will necessarily continue into the future is often a mistake.

The schematic suggests that *the key to successful style management is to be a contrarian*. When equity market participants universally view investing in a particular company as a waste of time, and the trend in the company's prospects is definitely downward, it may mean that the stock may be worth examining. Similarly, when market participants consider a stock to be a *core* holding that should be a central position in *every* portfolio, that may mean the stock is actually a sell candidate.

I mentioned that the equity market is probably a good discounter of investor perceptions or expectations at any point in time, but that those expectations will necessarily change because investors will not be able to judge a company's future prospects with complete certainty. If market participants seem to universally agree that a particular stock is a core holding that will definitely outperform the market, then any reevaluation of this obviously optimistic view must be more pessimistic. Similarly, if market participants universally agree that a stock is a "dog" that no one should ever own, then any reevaluation of future events must be more optimistic.

Thus, combining the idea that investor expectations are constantly changing with the Earnings Expectations Life Cycle suggests that the key to investment success is contrarian investing. Although the term contrarian is usually reserved for value managers, it actually applies to both growth and value managers. Traditional investment literature discusses contrarians as buyers of a stock that is decidedly out-of-favor. In fact, note that the first stage on the Earnings Expectations Life Cycle is termed contrarians. The Life Cycle suggests that the key to being a successful value manager is indeed contrarian buying, and that value managers might underperform when they buy stocks too early.

A recent example of value managers buying an industry group too early occurred during late 1992 when value-oriented investors began to overweight drug stocks within their portfolios. Drug stocks had begun to significantly underperform the overall equity market and, as a result, began to appear on relative valuation screens based on price/earnings ratios. Unfortunately, stock prices, being anticipatory, tend to fall faster than do analyst expectations for earnings. The result was P/E ratios that appeared depressed because a lower stock price was compared to analyst forecasts that were still optimistic. P/E ratios subsequently expanded, however, as analysts caught up to the pessimism that the market had been anticipating, and as the E began to erode. Thus, value managers' overweighted drug positions underperformed.

I have called the effect that causes stocks like the drug stocks in the prior example to appear temporarily undervalued the *valuation mirage*, (Bernstein, 1992). One buys a stock believing it to be of great value; however, the value is ephemeral and the investment underperforms. When value managers buy too early, it is usually because they have succumbed to the valuation mirage.

Figure 3.7 shows the valuation mirage by portraying consensus projected five-year earnings growth rates for the drug industry through time. One can see how dramatically earnings expectations

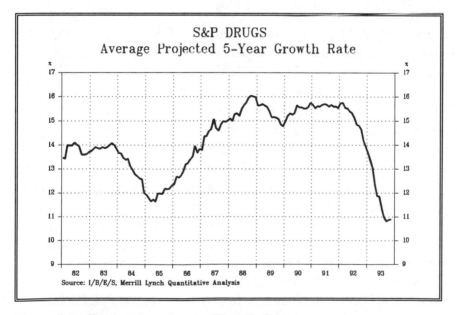

Figure 3.7 Expectations for the Drug Industry

for the drug group fell during 1993 as the valuation mirage dissipated.

Growth managers should also attempt to be contrarians; however, they should concentrate on being contrarian *sellers* rather than contrarian buyers. It's actually relatively easy to find growth stocks. Today, one can screen databases for companies that have superior growth characteristics, and again, if information is readily available, then the risk is that the information may already be incorporated into the stock price.

The difficult aspect to growth stock investing is uncovering when the growth characteristics that everyone can easily uncover will disappear. Given the earlier comments regarding the Earnings Expectations Life Cycle and why contrarians are usually successful investors, growth stock fundamentals usually erode when the consensus is sure that the company is infallible. Successful growth stock managers, therefore, usually look to sell when the consensus is most enthusiastic.

There has been much discussion over the past several years among institutional investors regarding transaction costs, or how much actually trading a stock detracts from theoretical performance. Suppose one decides to buy 1,000 shares of a stock that sells for $20 per share. On paper, one would have a $20,000 position. However, in reality, the demand for the stock may be quite high, and a 1,000 share buy order may force the stock price up in order to attract additional sellers. The order may be filled with 500 shares at $20 per share and 500 shares at $20.25, and while the paper portfolio has a $20,000 cost, the actual portfolio has a $20,125 cost. Obviously, this is a simple example, but this can be a significant problem when one considers the amount of trading within an institutional portfolio.

The Earnings Expectations Life Cycle suggests that contrarians not only tend to perform well because they are buying low and selling high, but also because they are the liquidity providers to the marketplace. If the contrarian is buying when everyone else is selling, or if the contrarian is selling when everyone else is buying, then the contrarian is the one in the earlier example who must be enticed by the extra \$0.25 per share to sell. Thus, the transaction cost problem described in the example is the contrarian's gain.

The Life Cycle, therefore, suggests that a transaction cost problem may be a function of poor timing of stock selection. Transaction costs themselves may be only a symptom of the larger problem, namely poor timing of buy/sell decisions. By definition, the contrarian should have lower transaction costs, and lower transaction costs mean added performance.

This chapter makes it all sound remarkably easy to be a contrarian. However, Shefrin and Statman (1993) have recently discussed why investors are not contrarians even when they may know that it is indeed better to be one. They believe that most investors are actually *conventionals* (the opposite of a contrarian) who make cognitive errors regarding popular stocks. In addition, such errors are hard to avoid even by sophisticated investors. By investing in stocks of "good" companies, they argue, investors remove much of the responsibility and potential blame from themselves for an investment that does not succeed. The management, the market, etc. can all be blamed for ruining a "good" company. In reality, "good" companies often have lower expected returns. However, the aversion to taking responsibility leads to faulty assessments of expected return. One extremely important point they make is that, by definition, there can't be too many contrarians simply because they would then be conventionals.

◆ Summary

- ◆ The equity market prices securities based on perception, not reality.

- ◆ Fundamental research that gauges consensus expectations may actually be of little value to investors.

- ◆ Insightful analysts will try to predict earnings surprises and the direction of revisions to consensus expectations.

- ◆ Earnings surprises are more likely to happen when the consensus forms a uniform viewpoint.

♦ The Earnings Expectations Life Cycle is a depiction of the various stages through which earnings expectations travel.

♦ Growth managers tend to be high-expectation managers. The ability to successfully undertake contrarian selling tends to separate good from bad growth stock managers.

♦ Value managers tend to be low-expectations managers. The ability to successfully undertake contrarian buying tends to separate good from bad value managers.

♦ Contrarians tend to outperform not only because they "buy low/sell high," but because they are the liquidity providers to the marketplace.

♦ Lower transaction costs translate to better performance. However, transaction cost problems may be a symptom of poor timing of stock selection.

♦ It sounds easy to be a contrarian, however, psychological factors make it quite difficult.

◆ Notes

1. David Dremen, *The New Contrarian Investment Strategy* (New York: Random House, 1982).
2. Robert D. Arnott, "The Use and Misuse of Consensus Earnings," *Journal of Portfolio Management*, 1985, vol. 11, no. 3, pp. 18–27, and Gary A. Benesh and Pamela P. Peterson, "On the Relation Between Earnings Changes, Analysts' Forecasts and Stock Price Fluctuations," *Financial Analysts Journal*, 1986, vol. 42, no. 6, pp. 29–39.
3. Peter L. Bernstein, "Growth Companies vs. Growth Stocks," *Harvard Business Review*, September/October 1956.
4. Eugene Hawkins, "Growth Stocks vs. Cyclicals: Some Important Differences in the Factors Affecting Price Performance, unpublished paper, 1985, and Michael E. Solt and Meir Statman, "Good Companies, Bad Stocks," *Journal of Portfolio Management*, 1989, vol. 15, no. 4, pp. 39–44.
5. Robert Hagin, "An Examination of the Torpedo Effect (or, Why the Equity Market Has a Low P/E Bias)," Paper presented at the Institute for Quantitative Research in Finance, Fall 1984, and Robert Hagin,

"The Torpedo Effect: The Subtle Risk of High Expected Growth," Paper presented at the Institute for Quantitative Research in Finance, Fall 1991.
6. Avner Arbel, Steven Carvell, and Paul Strebel, "Giraffes, Institutions and Neglected Firms," *Financial Analysts Journal*, 1983, vol. 39, no. 3, pp. 57–63.

◆ References

Bernstein, Richard, "Revisiting the Earnings Expectations Life Cycle," *Merrill Lynch Quantitative Viewpoint*, August 13, 1991.

Bernstein, Richard, "Avoid Valuation 'Mirages,' " *Merrill Lynch Quantitative Viewpoint*, July 14, 1992.

Bernstein, Richard, "The Earnings Expectations Life Cycle," *Financial Analysts Journal*, March/April 1993, pp. 90–93.

Elton, Edwin J., Gruber, Martin J., and Gultekin, Mustafa N., "Capital Market Efficiency and Expectations Data," I/B/E/S Working Paper, 1979, and "Expectations and Share Prices," *Management Science*, vol. 27, no. 9, September 1991.

Shefrin, Hersh, and Statman, Meir, "A Behavioral Framework for Expected Stock Returns," Presented at the Institute for Quantitative Research in Finance, October 1993.

PART II

4

Growth vs. Value

*I*f investors did not believe in market segmentation prior to the 1980s, chances are that they did by the end of the decade. During the 1980s, there were periods during which certain groups of stocks significantly outperformed the overall equity market, while other groups seriously under-performed. Although not unprecedented, that 1980s performance dichotomy appears to have removed the idea that all stocks move in tandem from most institutional investors' minds.

Figure 4.1, duplicated from Chapter 1, shows the performance of the S&P Capital Goods Index relative to that of the S&P Consumer Goods Index. As pointed out earlier, it is a dramatic example of how different sets of stocks performed during the 1980s. During that period, the price return of the S&P Consumer Goods Index was about 411 percent from December 1979 to December 1989, while the Capital Goods Index was up only 140 percent. For comparison, the S&P 500 was up 223 percent over the same period.

Institutional investors began to search for reasons why the consumer sectors of the equity market were performing so well, while the industrial sectors performed so poorly. In retrospect (and those may be the key words within this chapter), it was found that stocks within the consumer sector had certain common growth characteristics, while most of the stocks in the industrial sector did not. The only question regarding the industrial sector was whether the stocks had underperformed so dramatically that they were cheaper than the value of the companies' underlying assets, in other words, whether they were undervalued stocks.

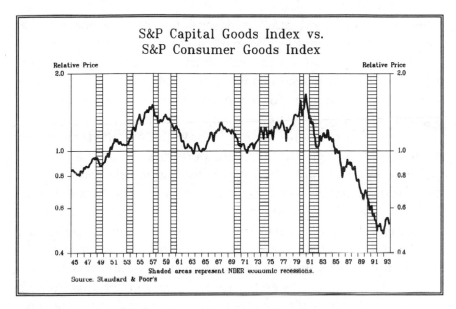

Figure 4.1 Capital Goods vs. Consumer Goods

It is interesting to note that the performance dichotomy became so wide during the 1980s that it encouraged many traditional
efficient market enthusiasts to support some element of market
segmentation. For example, William Sharpe (1992) helped to develop a set of growth and value indexes, and used those style
indices to help explain manager performance.

Thus, although the concepts of growth and value investing
have long been used within the investment community, they
gained considerable attention within the past ten years, and institutional investors now consider these strategies to be integral parts
of their investment philosophies. Two things may have contributed
to that relatively new-found attention. First, the performance spread
between managers who invested in consumer-oriented, growth
stocks and those who invested in more cyclical, value-oriented
stocks became so wide that some managers portrayed themselves
as growth managers simply to avoid the connotation of offering a
losing strategy to potential clients. Anecdotally, it was hard to find
a start-up money management firm during the late 1980s that por-

trayed itself as a "hard core" value-oriented manager for fear that it would not be invited to take part in money manager searches.

Second, the pension consultant business began to expand during the 1980s, and pension consultants tend to pigeonhole or categorize money managers for comparison purposes. For example, it might not be fair to compare a manager who only invests in growth companies with one who invests in only undervalued situations. In fact, even though the absolute performance of the growth-oriented manager might be higher, the value-oriented manager might actually be the better money manager of the two. It is possible that the worst growth-oriented manager's absolute performance might be better than the best value-oriented manager simply because the overall universe of growth stocks outperformed the overall universe of value stocks. Pension consultants, in their roles as consumer advocates, search for good managers relative to their peers. Why should a plan sponsor pay a hundred-basis-point fee to a manager whose performance is better than that of the S&P 500 simply because the universe of stocks from which the manager chooses is outperforming, but yet the manager is not outperforming the universe? In effect, that manager would be providing negative value. Thus, for value managers, the demarcation became important in order to demonstrate their money management skills, even though their absolute performance generally was not on a par with that of growth managers.

This initial chapter on style management focuses on these two dominant investment styles within the institutional arena, their definitions, their characteristics, and why and when each might outperform the other strategy or even the overall equity market.

Within the context of the Earnings Expectations Life Cycle as shown in Chapter 3, value managers were defined as low-expectations managers because they tend to search for investments among stocks that are out of favor. The assumption behind value investing is that the consensus views a company overly pessimistically, and that the stock's valuation will improve once the consensus realizes its mistake. Value managers, therefore, usually search for stocks that sell below the worth of a company's assets or below the value of its future growth prospects. The skill to value investing is in timing a change of heart in the consensus. One can easily buy a stock that has been underperforming and claim that it is an unusual value only to see the stock price continue to decline. When value managers underperform, it is usually because they have bought too early.

Growth stock managers were defined as high-expectation managers, who prefer to search for investments among stocks that have a proven superior track record of earnings growth. Growth stock investors usually pay a high premium to hold such stocks because the market realizes the superior qualities of the company. The assumption behind growth stock investing is that the market will continue to reward the superior grower. The key to success for a growth stock manager is realizing when that superior growth pattern may deteriorate. The stock's price would surely fall should investors realize that the premium they paid was for nothing. Thus, growth stock investors must be careful not to hold a stock too long.

Some portray value investors as the insightful ones, while painting growth stock investors as patsies. For example, Jacques and Wood (1993) state that value strategies such as low price/earnings outperform through time because higher P/E stocks are owned by growth managers who simply fall in love with their stocks and have no concept of a stock's intrinsic value. Value managers, they imply, are insightful bargain hunters, while growth managers simply play the greater fool's game. Both portraits may be inaccurate. Both value and growth managers have equal opportunity to be insightful investors or patsies. The insightful value manager actually will buy later than his or her peers, and the insightful growth manager will sell sooner. The patsy value manager buys too early, and the patsy growth manager hangs on too long. Neither group of managers has the right to laugh at the other.

Value and growth managers can attempt to be insightful any number of ways, and a question often asked is, "What exactly is 'growth' and 'value'?" The definition or strategy one uses is critical to one's performance and to one's understanding of why these styles perform the way they do. Value is relatively easy to define, but growth is slightly more nebulous. In addition, one must consider whether the two styles are completely mutually exclusive;

whether growth stocks can be undervalued or whether value stocks can have superior growth. Should a stock never be in both a growth and a value manager's portfolio?

Table 4.1 shows the price returns for two different types of growth- and value-oriented indices that we developed at Merrill Lynch. One will note that the performance of these indices is quite different despite that they are supposed to measure similar investment styles.

The first set of indices measures the change in net asset value of eighteen large and well-known mutual funds (nine value/nine growth). These indices attempt to gauge actual manager performance as opposed to stock performance. The advantage to these indices is that they show the historical performance of actual portfolios, rather than of potential universes of stocks from which managers can choose. Their disadvantage is that the managers within the indices may not be able to outperform a style benchmark and may detract from the true style performance, or they might be superior managers and add to the true performance. In either case, the probability that manager performance is identical to true style performance is relatively low. Some observers assume that manager performance is identical or should coincide with stock universe performance measures. The comparison of the performance of these indices with those of the more true version suggest that manager performance is not identical to that of the style itself.

Table 4.1 Growth and Value Index Performance

Year	Growth Funds	Growth Stocks	Value Funds	Value Stocks
1987	−14.7%	15.4%	−10.4%	−2.5%
1988	8.2	5.9	11.4	33.4
1989	19.6	29.8	6.9	18.4
1990	−8.6	−6.8	−13.1	−20.5
1991	28.9	31.7	15.3	52.3
1992	−1.8	3.0	6.2	19.2
1993	3.0	10.2	6.9	21.8

Source: Merrill Lynch Quantitative Analysis

Table 4.2 lists the names of the funds that are included in
these indices. These funds were chosen primarily because they have
been in existence for some time, and are well-known growth and
value funds and, therefore, the risk of a fund "cheating" and
switching styles through time was low.

The second set measures the average price returns of the fifty
stocks within the S&P 500 with the highest projected five-year
earnings growth rates and the fifty stocks in the S&P 500 with the
highest earnings yield. (High earnings yield is the inverse of low
price/earnings; i.e., E/P instead of P/E. Companies that might
have an infinite P/E because they don't have earnings would simply have an earnings yield of 0 percent. Thus, it is more helpful
within quantitative models because it produces a smoother distribution.) The fifty high expected growth stocks are used as a proxy
for a "pure" growth portfolio, while the fifty earnings yield stocks
are used as a proxy for a "pure" value portfolio. The term "pure"
is used because the portfolios are those within the S&P 500 that
are made up of the companies that show the most extreme values
of the particular characteristic. There are no overlays for quality,
size, or other considerations discussed in later chapters. If a portfolio manager had a fifty-stock portfolio, any differences in portfolio
composition from the "pure" portfolio might be attributable to the
portfolio manager's subjective judgment, and could impart biases

Table 4.2   Constituents of Mutual Fund Growth and Value Indices

Growth Funds	*Value Funds*
Amcap Fund	Affiliated Fund
American Capital Pace	American Mutual
Fidelity Destiny	Dreyfus Fund
GE S&S Program	Investment Company of America
Growth Fund of America	Mutual Shares
Nicholas Fund	Pioneer II
Smith Barney Shearson Appreciation Fund	Putnam Growth & Income
T. Rowe Price Growth Stock	Washington Mutual
Twentieth Century Select	Windsor Fund

into the portfolio that have little to do with the particular style itself. Thus, one difference between manager performance and style universe performance is the active stock selection choices of the managers within the index.

A set of indices have been recently constructed by S&P/Barra, and are based on price/book value ratios. Growth is defined in these indices as the half of the S&P 500 (or 250 stocks) with the highest price/book value ratios, while value is defined as the half of the S&P 500 with the lowest price/book value ratios. An important point regarding these indices is that they force the definitions of growth and value to be mutually exclusive; e.g., a stock is either in the top half of price/book value or it is not. In addition, the growth index constructed by S&P/Barra is comprised of stocks that have shown superior growth, not necessarily stocks that will show superior growth.

In Chapter 3, we introduced the earnings "torpedo" and that concept's role within the Earnings Expectations Life Cycle. Torpedoes are usually preceded by a period during which investors overwhelmingly agree that the particular stock will be a superior grower. Hagin (1991) has pointed out that there is a higher probability of earnings torpedoes among stocks with higher price/earnings ratios. The probability increases because expectations simply get too optimistic, and the slightest disappointment triggers investors to sell. Hagin's findings are probably based on the same effect found by Solt and Statman mentioned earlier ("good" companies make "bad" stocks). Although the S&P/Barra indices are based on price/book value and not price/earnings, a study relating torpedoes to high price/book value ratios would probably give similar results. Thus, the S&P/Barra growth index, and other such indices built upon mutually exclusive groups, may have a built-in "torpedo" effect that might make it an easier benchmark for managers to outperform.

In fact, even using our "pure" indices, performance can change dramatically depending on the particular strategy that one employs to attempt to define growth or value. Figures 4.2 to 4.5 that follow highlight the performance of the fifty stocks within the S&P 500 relative to the equal-weighted S&P 500 according to four common

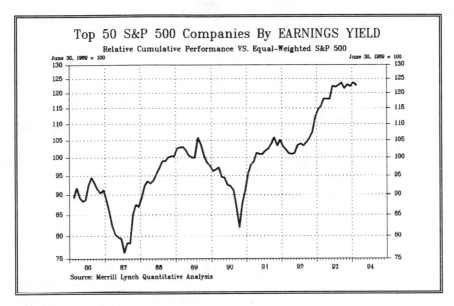

Figure 4.2   High Earnings Yield

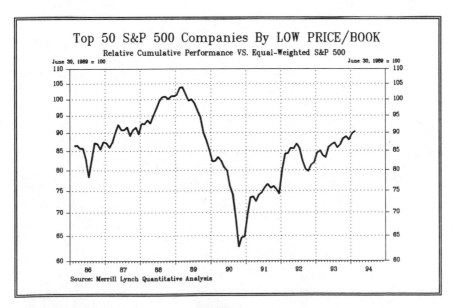

Figure 4.3   Low Price-to-Book Value

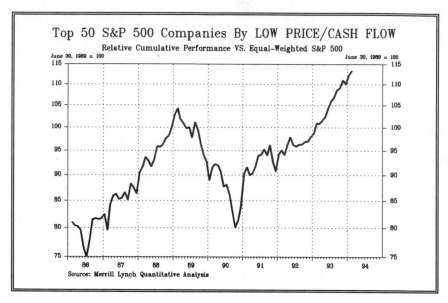

Figure 4.4 Low Price-to-Cash Flow

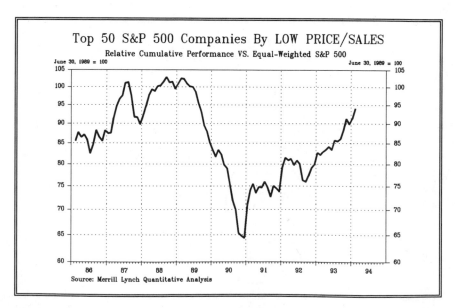

Figure 4.5 Low Price-to-Sales

value-related characteristics. (Note: The equal-weighted S&P 500 is a performance benchmark that is comprised of the S&P 500 universe of stocks. However, instead of share-weighting the con- stituents as S&P does, the companies receive identical weights. The advantage of the equal-weighted S&P 500 to the actual S&P 500 is that the equal-weighted S&P 500 contains little size bias, while the actual S&P 500 is heavily influenced by larger stocks. While large capitalization stocks such as Exxon, IBM, and WalMart greatly influence the actual S&P 500, they have the identical influence as that of the other 497 stocks within the equal-weighted S&P 500.)

Visually, the relative performances of these value-oriented portfolios seem to be quite similar. They perform well from 1986 to 1989, poorly in 1990, and well again from 1991 to 1993. How- ever, Table 4.3 shows year-by-year performance, and one can see that the definition that one might use to define a universe of value stocks can have a significant impact on performance. Excluding the Dividend Discount Model (DDM), there was an average of 8.7 percentage points between the best and the worst performing value portfolio each year. Thus, a portfolio manager could have easily gone from significantly outperforming a value benchmark to sig- nificantly underperforming one depending on the definition of value in any particular year.

The Dividend Discount Model (DDM), the last column in the table, is a value-oriented quantitative model that attempts to value stocks based on the present value of anticipated dividends and earnings growth. These models are generally based on the same

Table 4.3   Performance of Value Characteristics

Year	EPS Yield	Low P/B	Low P/CF	Low P/S	DDM
1987	−2.5%	4.8%	8.1%	4.2%	2.4%
1988	33.4	30.4	34.0	28.1	15.1
1989	18.4	2.6	12.7	4.1	20.7
1990	−20.5	−35.1	−22.8	−35.5	−15.0
1991	52.3	50.9	42.5	50.9	30.4
1992	19.2	23.5	20.7	21.1	1.3
1993	21.8	19.8	25.4	25.6	5.7

Source: Merrill Lynch Quantitative Analysis

formula as the yield-to-maturity calculation for a bond, except that, instead of the known coupon payments one might receive from a bond, one uses analyst estimates for future dividends that might be received. The historical performance of the fifty stocks within the S&P 500 that have been the most attractive according to the Merrill Lynch DDM is presented in Figure 4.6, and one will note that the model's performance is very different from the performance figures just shown for other value-oriented stock-picking methods.

That performance discrepancy between the DDM and other value-oriented characteristics is largely attributable to the "valuation mirage" mentioned in Chapter 3. Stock prices tend to fall faster than do analyst expectations, and stocks will temporarily look quite attractive within the DDM when that happens because the future potential cash flows appear to be obtainable at a cheaper current price. Unfortunately, such valuation mirages are usually corrected by the analysts lowering their estimates, and not by the stock price rising. The DDM's relative underperformance during the 1992–93

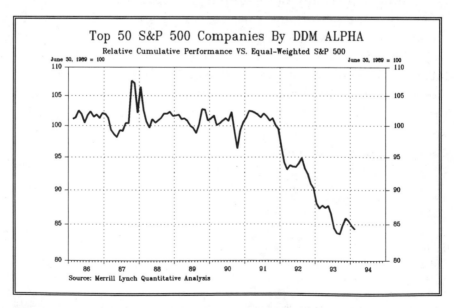

Figure 4.6 Relative Performance of the DDM

period can largely be attributed to that effect, as many consumer growth stocks experienced significant valuation mirages.

Table 4.4 shows the correlations of the twelve-month returns of the various value-oriented stock-picking methods shown. Correlations are calculated based on performance rather than on index values because correlations based on index values may be unrealistically high. Despite market segmentation, equity returns, in general, tend to be positive, and therefore, indices tend to trend upward, and correlations may appear quite positive because of that underlying trend. Performance tends to detrend the returns and may give a more accurate appraisal of the comovement among the returns. Note that the DDM correlated less well with the other value-oriented characteristics, and that the correlations among the others vary. This shows that the definition that one chooses in defining value can indeed make a large difference in one's perspective of investment success.

Figures 4.7 to 4.10 show the relative performance of roughly the fifty stocks within the S&P 500 with the highest projected five-year earnings growth rates, the largest upward revisions in consensus earnings estimates, the highest probability of earnings surprise, and the fastest earnings momentum (year-to-year percent change in actual earnings). Unlike the performance of the value-oriented group, the performance among growth-oriented strategies even visually varies, again demonstrating that the method that one might choose to implement a growth or value strategy can have a significant impact on one's performance. Table 4.5 shows the annual performance numbers.

Table 4.4 Value Characteristic Correlations—12-Month Returns

	EPS Yield	Low P/B	Low P/CF	Low P/S	DDM
EPS Yield	—				
Low P/B	0.81	—			
Low P/CF	0.86	0.96	—		
Low P/S	0.78	0.98	0.97	—	
DDM	0.72	0.78	0.87	0.80	—

Source: Merrill Lynch Quantitative Analysis

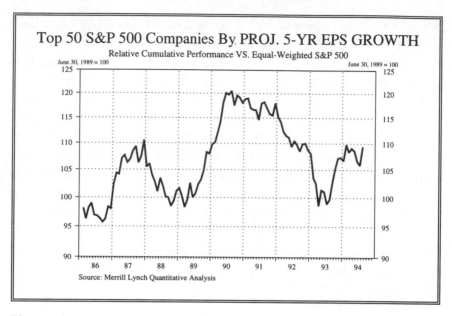

Figure 4.7   Projected 5-Year Earnings Growth

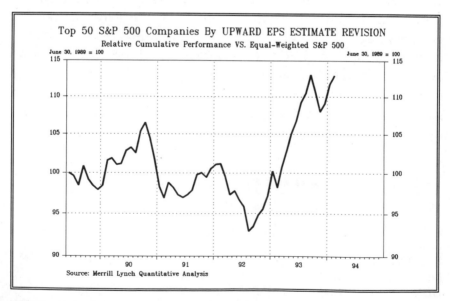

Figure 4.8   Estimate Revision

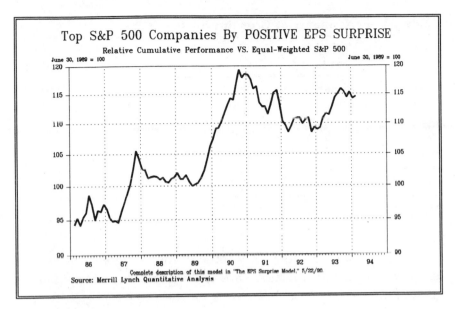

Figure 4.9 Earnings Surprise

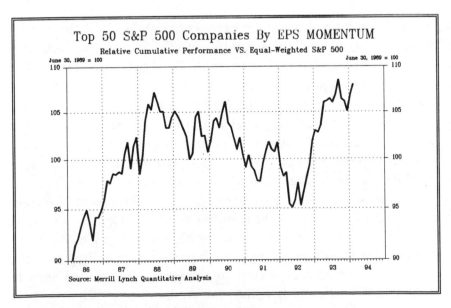

Figure 4.10 Earnings Momentum

Table 4.5   Performance of Growth Characteristics

Year	Hi Proj. Growth	EPS Est. Rev.	Pos. EPS Surp.	EPS Momentum
1987	15.4%	na	9.6%	10.4%
1988	5.9	na	12.5	18.0
1989	29.8	na	27.4	17.3
1990	−6.8	−11.5	−4.8	−14.9
1991	31.7	30.4	26.0	33.5
1992	3.0	7.9	7.9	11.9
1993	10.2	25.4	17.7	15.2

Source: Merrill Lynch Quantitative Analysis

It may not be obvious why some of these strategies presented as growth-oriented strategies are indeed growth-oriented. Most growth managers probably investigate the projected growth rates and earnings momentum of the companies that they buy, but earnings surprise and earnings estimate revisions may be less commonly used. They are included in this group of growth strategies because they tend to perform better during the equity market's growth-driven periods.

As mentioned before, the product bought and sold within the equity market is nominal earnings growth, and the abundance or scarcity of that product will determine equity style rotation. When growth is scarce, strategies such as earnings surprise tend to work better because the strategy highlights to the market that the particular stock offers an additional amount of growth. Investors then flock to the stock to buy the extra unit of available growth much as a thirsty person would rush toward water in a desert. Thus, such strategies are better classified as growth-oriented strategies.

Figures 4.11 and 4.12 highlight the relationship between growth and value cycles and earnings surprises. Figure 4.11 shows the relative performance between the high earnings yield portfolio (value) and the high projected growth portfolio (growth) previously mentioned. The relative performance carves out cycles of growth- and value-driven periods within the equity market. Clearly, there have been periods during which it might have been advantageous

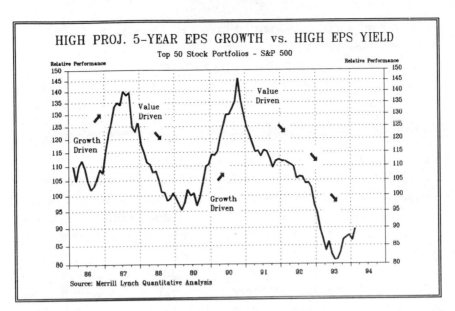

Figure 4.11 Growth and Value Cycles

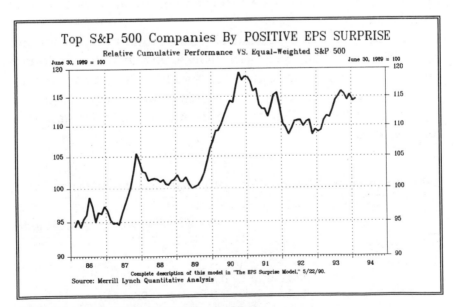

Figure 4.12 EPS Surprise Model Performance

to have been a growth-oriented investor, and others during which a value investor would have benefited.

Figure 4.12 again shows the performance of the Merrill Lynch Quantitative Analysis Earnings Surprise Model relative to the equal-weighted S&P 500. Note that the Earnings Surprise Model outperforms during periods depicted as growth-driven in Figure 4.11, and tends to perform less well during periods depicted as value-driven.

Table 4.6 shows the correlations of the twelve-month returns among these growth-oriented strategies. Note that the correlations are lower than those presented for the value-oriented strategies.

Well-defined universes of stocks may be preferable to define growth and value. General universes tend to be exclusive, that is, a stock is *either* growth or value, but cannot be both. Although manager universes may be preferable to indices based on mutually exclusive groups of stocks, one must allow for the positive or negative contribution that active management might make. Well-defined universes of stocks, however, are not necessarily mutually exclusive (a stock can be both growth and value), and are not affected by portfolio managers' contribution to or detraction from performance.

Given the relatively distinctive growth and value cycles present within historical stock performance, obviously the important question is whether one can forecast such cycles. In this section, we will discuss the factors that have historically influenced growth and value cycles and that can aid in attempting to forecast style relative performance.

Table 4.6 Growth Strategy Correlations—12-Month Returns

	Proj. Growth	Est. Revision	EPS Surprise	EPS Momentum
Proj. Growth	—			
Est. Revision	0.63	—		
EPS Surprise	0.85	0.87	—	
EPS Momentum	0.71	0.94	0.92	—

Source: Merrill-Lynch Quantitative Analysis

As mentioned, the abundance or scarcity of nominal earnings growth significantly influences the relative performance of market segments and style investing. That has certainly been true regarding the relative performance of growth and value managers' performance. Figure 4.13 compares the year-to-year percent change in S&P 500 earnings per share with the relative net asset value of our selected universes of growth and value mutual funds. During the 1980s, the relative performance of growth and value managers appeared to be inverse to the supply of earnings growth. As earnings growth becomes more scarce (from the peak to the trough of earnings momentum), growth managers will tend to outperform value managers. However, value managers have tended to outperform when earnings momentum has historically become more abundant (from the trough to the peak of earnings momentum).

Growth managers will tend to outperform as earnings momentum becomes scarce because growth itself becomes a scarce resource, and investors bid up the price of that scarcity. If only a few companies are growing, then investors will want to hold that small universe of stocks and will accordingly bid up the stocks'

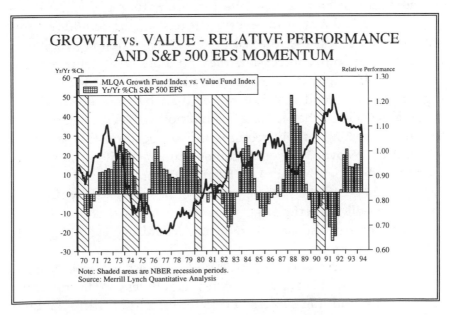

Figure 4.13 Earnings Momentum and Manager Performance

prices. However, value managers will tend to outperform as earnings growth becomes more abundant because investors may tend to increasingly comparison shop. If a larger number of companies grow, then why would one pay a high price for an abundant resource (remember our apples and diamonds example). Thus, forecasted earnings momentum might be one variable that an investor could use to forecast the cycles of growth and value.

It is somewhat ironic that "growth stock" investing is often portrayed as a very optimistic style of investing. Advertisements for growth funds often mention looking for America's growth stocks to lead the nation into the twenty-first century. However, growth stock investing actually may be a relatively pessimistic view of the world. Its underlying theme is that the economy will be so poor and the profits cycle so weak that investors much search out those few companies that might actually be able to grow in that environment. Value investing is actually the much more optimistic of the two strategies because its underlying theme is that everything is going to grow, so shop around for growth.

Most economic forecasts usually contain forecasts of earnings momentum, but professional investors are notoriously wary of the figures presented within an economic forecast. One should remember that changes in the forecast or the forecast figures relative to those made by other forecasters may be more important than the forecast itself. It may be more important to simply know that earnings momentum will improve rather than by how much. If the consensus believed that earnings would not recover, then a rotation to value investing simply requires the supposition that earnings will indeed recover. It then becomes immaterial if earnings momentum subsequently improves from −25 percent to +10 percent or from −25 percent to +25 percent. In either case, history suggests that value will outperform growth. If the forecast changes were becoming more pessimistic, then history would suggest that growth would outperform.

Value-oriented investing was quite successful through most of the 1960s and 1970s, but was considerably less so during much of the 1980s, and that success and failure might be attributable to inflation and disinflation.

Earlier, we mentioned the importance of the word "nominal" when discussing earnings growth, and that implies that inflation can play an important role in determining the cycles of growth and value investing. Inflation increases the level of earnings and, therefore, tends to cause investors to downplay the negatives related to a poorly managed company. Although the firm may be in trouble, rising inflation may bail out the firm by allowing it to simply raise prices. If obligations, such as debt, are relatively fixed, then inflation will make the "bad" company seem quite profitable.

In addition, investors search for investments with higher dividend yields during periods of rising inflation. During inflationary periods, it becomes more important to get as much return as one can as quickly as one can get it in order to quickly reinvest at still higher potential rates of return. Value-oriented investments tend to have higher dividend yields that provide the investor with more short-term return. That search for short-term return during periods of inflation causes investors to reallocate funds toward money market instruments in the fixed-income market and toward value-oriented investment within the equity market during periods of rising inflation.

Similarly, interest rates are another important factor to consider when attempting to forecast secular periods or cycles of growth and value investing. One should consider both the change in the level of interest rates and the slope of the yield curve. The level of interest rates affects stocks in terms of their durations or interest rate sensitivities, while the shape of the yield curve may be an implicit forecast within the financial market of future growth prospects.

Equity duration is discussed in more detail in Chapter 7, but it is a measure of a stock's interest rate sensitivity. Stocks with longer durations will tend to be more interest-rate sensitive than stocks with shorter durations. Duration is stated in years (and the adjectives long and short are used instead of high and low) because it measures not only how much return is expected from a stock or bond, but *when* it can be expected. In other words, two stocks may have identical expected total returns, say 10 percent. Stock A's total return is comprised of 7 percent capital appreciation and 3 percent yield, while stock B's total return is comprised solely of 10 percent capital appreciation. Although yield is relatively certain return, capital appreciation is relatively indefinite with respect to timing and amount. The present value of future cash flows decreases as interest rates rise and, therefore, if interest rates were to rise, stock A's price would probably outperform stock B's because stocks B's entire return is dependent on events that are further in the future than those associated with some proportion of the return of stock A. Stock A's dividend yield allows the investor to gain some near-term return that stock B does not offer. Thus, much the same way that T-Bills outperform T-Bonds during periods of rising interest rates, stock A has a shorter duration than does stock B. Of course, stock B would outperform stock A if interest rates were falling because the opposite of the preceding example would be true.

The mathematical derivation of equity duration is covered in Chapter 7, but for now there are two methods for calculating the duration of a stock. The first, more simple method is to simply take the inverse of a stock's dividend yield. Using that formula, stocks with high dividend yields would have short durations, while those with little or no dividend yield would have long durations. This is an intuitive method, and is useful in discussion, but is limited because it assumes that dividend policy is constant into the future. The growth stock that may not currently pay dividends is assumed to never pay dividends at any time in the future. Obviously, that assumption is somewhat unrealistic.

The second method for calculating equity duration is based on the Dividend Discount Model. The mathematics of bond duration are based on the yield-to-maturity formula, and the DDM can be viewed as solving for the "yield-to-maturity" of a stock, which is more commonly referred to as the expected return. However, if the formula for the DDM is similar to that of the bond's yield-to-maturity, then the derivative formula can be applied to the DDM to arrive at the duration of a stock. The advantage of this duration calculation is that future dividend payments and cash flows are not assumed to be constant as they are in the inverse of the dividend yield calculation. Assumptions can be made regarding growth stocks paying dividends in the future.

Table 4.7 shows the durations of several economic sectors and market segments. Note that the duration calculations do not change substantially for sectors that are usually higher dividend payers, such as Energy, Utilities, and "Defensive" stocks. Because they pay dividends and have relatively meager growth prospects, their long-term growth and cash flow patterns within the DDM practically do not change through time. Durations calculated using the fancier DDM-related or using the inverse of the dividend yield calculation virtually do not change because the future returns look like a perpetuity.

Durations differ dramatically, however, for sectors for which future growth and payout patterns are expected to change through time. In fact, the more the growth and payout assumptions change,

Table 4.7 Durations of Equity Sectors and Segments as of December 1993

Sector/Segment	DDM Duration	Inv. of Yield
Transportation	38.9	71.4
"Overvalued" Stocks	38.9	52.6
Credit Cyclicals	35.9	66.7
Technology	35.6	90.9
Consumer Cyclicals	32.8	55.6
Basic Industrials	32.6	40.0
"Small Stocks"	32.1	90.9
"Mid-Cap" Stocks	30.8	45.4
Conglomerates	30.1	38.5
Financial	29.8	38.5
Consumer Growth Staples	29.7	71.4
"Growth" Stocks	29.3	66.7
S&P 500	**28.5**	**40.0**
"Large" Stocks	28.2	38.5
Capital Goods	28.2	47.6
Consumer Staples	25.0	47.6
Energy	24.9	27.8
"Undervalued" Stocks	23.2	33.3
"Defensive" Stocks	22.3	21.7
Utilities	22.0	21.7

Source: Merrill Lynch Quantitative Analysis

the more different the two measures of duration will be. For example, the durations of "Small" and "Growth" stocks are measured quite differently depending on the method chosen.

It should not be surprising that growth stocks tend to have relatively high durations. A typical growth stock might be described as one with a higher-than-average P/E or P/B that pays little or no dividends, while a value stock might be described as one with a relatively low P/E or P/B that generally pays dividends. For the growth stock, the higher P/E means that the stock price is discounting events farther into the future, while the lack of a dividend suggests no interim payments. On the other hand, the value stock's low P/E suggests that the time horizon being discounted into the stock's price is relatively short, while the higher dividend payments suggest interim returns.

Table 4.8 highlights the DDM-related durations for fifty stock portfolios formed using various growth and value strategies. The average value strategy portfolio had a duration of 24.9 years, while the duration of the average growth strategy portfolio was indeed longer, at 29.9 years. The equal-weighted S&P 500 had a duration of about 27.8 years at the time.

Although not a perfect example, the relationship between high-yield or "junk bonds" and government bonds might help explain why value investing performs well during periods of inflation and/ or rising interest rates. From the economic perspective, junk bonds outperform governments during periods of rising inflation simply because it is harder to go bankrupt, as fixed obligations can be paid off with cheaper, inflated dollars. They underperform during periods

Table 4.8 Duration of Growth and Value Strategies

Value		Growth	
EPS Yield	21.0	EPS Surprise	27.7
DDM	23.0	EPS Momentum	28.2
P/S	26.7	Proj. Growth	31.1
P/CF	26.8	Est. Revision	32.7
P/B	27.1		
Average	**24.9**	**Average**	**29.9**

Source: Merrill Lynch Quantitative Analysis

of falling interest rates because interest rates often fall because the economy is getting weaker. If the economy is getting weaker, then the risk of bankruptcy tends to go up, and investors move toward safer investments.

From the more mathematical duration perspective, junk bonds outperform as interest rates rise because they are shorter-duration bonds. Their name—high yield—indicates that their coupon payments are higher than those of quality or government bonds. Thus, as interest rates rise, the shorter-duration "junk bonds" outperform the government bond or the 30-year zero-coupon bond. When interest rates fall, the zero-coupon would outperform the other bonds.

As interest rates rise, the risk of bankruptcy decreases, and the undervalued, ignored, and often higher-yielding stock will tend to outperform the zero-yielding growth stock. However, when interest rates fall, the opposite would generally be true.

Harvey (1989, 1993) has pointed out that the slope of the yield curve is an accuracte forecast of future economic growth. It follows then that the slope of the yield curve is also quite an important indicator for growth and value investors. The slope of goverment bond yield curve that measures the current yield-to-maturity of T-Bonds and the current discount rate of T-Bills can be thought of as an implicit forecast of future nominal growth rates. If the future is expected to be less robust, then the yield curve will generally take on what is known as an inverted shape, meaning that T-Bill rates are generally higher than T-Bond rates. The curve might become inverted for two reasons. First, the Federal Reserve might have raised short-term interest rates because they fear the risk of inflation. By raising short-term rates, they hope to begin to constrain borrowing power which will, in turn, slow the economy. Second, longer-term investors might buy long-term bonds because they believe that nominal growth rates will be slow or that inflation is not a concern. Such buying would raise the price of bonds, but lower their yields. Thus, an inverted yield curve, whether it be inverted because the Fed has raised short-term rates or because longer-term investors are not fearful of future rising growth and interest rates, generally signals a poorer economic environment ahead.

A steep yield curve, or one in which T-Bill rates are generally lower than T-Bond rates, signals a view of a more robust future. That view could be because the Fed has lowered short-term rates in an attempt to stimulate the economy, or it could be because long-term investors are beginning to fear that future growth may be too strong, which would force interest rates higher as borrowing pressures mounted. If longer-term investors sold bonds because of such fears, then bond prices would decline and yields would rise.

If the contentions that the yield curve is a forecast of future economic conditions and that growth strategies outperform as conditions worsen are correct, then one might expect growth strategies to have outperformed when the yield curve was inverted. If value strategies outperform as conditions improve (whether on a real or nominal basis), then value strategies should have worked better when the yield curve was steep.

Figure 4.14 shows that the relationship just described between growth, value, and the slope of the yield curve appears to hold. It compares the relative net asset value of the eighteen growth and value mutual funds with the three-month T-Bill to thirty-year T-

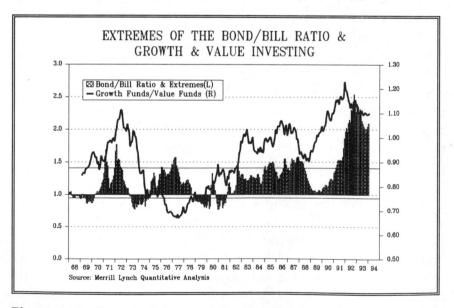

Figure 4.14 Growth, Value, and the Slope of the Yield Curve

Bond ratio. When that ratio is greater than 1.0, it indicates that the yield curve is steep and that the bond rate is higher than the bill rate. When it is less than 1.0, it indicates that the yield curve is inverted and that the bill rate is higher than the bond rate.

The relative fund performance seems to adhere to the preceding description, although it is not straightforward. The extreme values relating to the slope of the yield curve seem to be more important than the slope itself. There may actually be four phases though which the yield curve changes its slope, and growth and value each seem to outperform during two of them. Starting with a yield curve that is changing from flat to inverted, growth will tend to outperform value because investors realize that the Fed is actually trying to choke off the economic expansion. Next, as the slope changes from extremely inverted to flat, growth will still outperform value because investors now believe that the Fed realizes that they may have been too restrictive and is beginning to ease short-term interest rates because the economy is in recession. Value will begin to outperform as the slope of the yield curve changes from flat to steep. Here, investors realize that the Fed is now trying to make a concerted effort to stimulate the economy. Value will also outperform as the slope goes from extremely steep to flat because investors will believe that the Fed is reacting to the strength within the economy and is trying to slow the economic expansion. Value will continue to outperform until the slope of the yield curve is flat. Beyond that, we return to the starting phase in this example. Table 4.9 summarizes the slope of the yield curve and growth and value performance.

One of the best indicators of economic confidence comes from corporate America, but it is a contrary signal. If corporate man-

Table 4.9 Growth and Value Performance and the Slope of the Yield Curve

Yield Curve	Style Performance	Rationale
Flat to Inverted	Growth Outperforms	Choking Economy
Inverted to Flat	Growth Outperforms	Overly Restrictive
Flat to Steep	Value Outperforms	Stimulative
Steep to Flat	Value Outperforms	Too Easy

agement is relatively uncertain and wary of future economic prospects, that suggests that one should be a value investor. However, when corporate management becomes sanguine regarding the economy, that historically has suggested that a recession is on the horizon, and that investors should shift toward growth stocks. One might want to think of an Earnings Expectations Life Cycle for the economy and corporate management. When management is overly pessimistic, then the economy might be at six o'clock on the cycle, but when they are overly confident, then the economy might be at midnight.

The dividend payout ratio of the overall S&P 500 is generally a good indicator of over-optimism or over-pessimism among corporate managers. Payout ratios are calculated simply as the dollar amount of dividend divided by the dollar amount of earnings. If a company earned $10 per share and paid out $4 in dividends, then its dividend payout ratio would be 40 percent ($4/$10).

There has been a tremendous amount of academic literature on the "signaling" effect of dividends, or literally the signal regarding management's view of the future that an increase or decrease of the dividend sends to the marketplace. A dividend increase is obviously a positive signal, while a decrease is a negative one. Corporate management may be wary to change dividend policy because of that powerful signaling effect. They may not want to be too quick to raise dividend payments for fear of having to lower them soon thereafter. Conversely, they may not want to cut dividends until they are sure that they must because they may not want to send such a negative signal to the market if the company's problems are only short-lived. Their hesitancy, as a group, to shift dividend policy makes the dividend payout ratio a relatively reliable contrary indicator. Figure 4.15 shows the relationship between the growth in earnings per share and dividends per share for the S&P 500. Earnings growth is much more variable probably because of that hesitancy to change dividend policy.

Figure 4.16 shows the relationship between the dividend payout ratio for the S&P 500 and the relative net asset values of growth and value managers. Although not a perfect relationship, one can see that value has historically outperformed growth after the div-

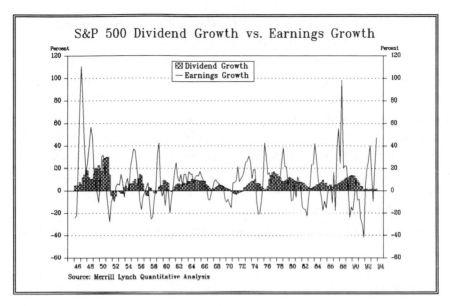

Figure 4.15   Growth Rates of S&P 500 EPS and DPS

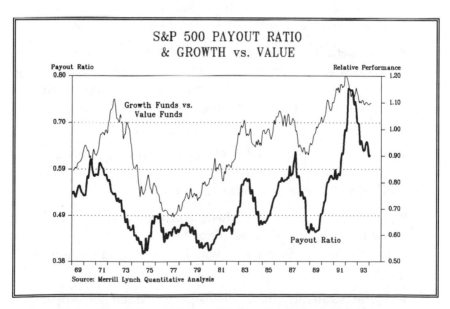

Figure 4.16   Growth and Value and Dividend Payout Ratios

idend payout ratio peaks, while growth has outperformed historically when the dividend payout ratio troughs.

Given that earnings tend to be more variable than are dividends, monitoring the dividend payout ratio is a method for monitoring "normalized" earnings. In other words, if the payout ratio is toward the bottom of its historical range, that implies that earnings have been quite strong, and the odds are that earnings will weaken. Weaker earnings imply accentuating a growth stock orientation. However, if the dividend payout ratio is toward the high end of its historical range, that implies that earnings have been relatively weak, and the odds are that earnings growth will improve. An improving earnings scenario suggests a value orientation.

◆ Summary

♦ The combination of a severe segmentation in market performance and the advent of the pension consultant led investors to truly believe in market segmentation and style investing by the end of the 1980s. The primary styles upon which investors focused were growth and value.

♦ The definition one chooses to define, or strategy one chooses to implement a growth or value strategy can significantly alter one's performance or perception of whether growth or value is the superior strategy at any point in time.

♦ Contrary to popular belief, growth investing actually requires a rather pessimistic view of the world, while value investing is a more optimistic view.

♦ Growth strategies have historically tended to outperform value strategies when earnings momentum waned, interest rates fell, the yield curve was inverted, and payout ratios rose.

♦ Value strategies have historically tended to outperform growth strategies when earnings momentum improved, interest rates rose, the yield curve was steep, and payout ratios fell.

◆ *References*

Bernstein, Richard, "A Bond Investor's Guide to Equity and Duration," *Merrill Lynch Quantitative Viewpoint*. February 25, 1992.

Bernstein, Richard, "The Black Widow of Valuation," *Merrill Lynch Quantitative Viewpoint*, February 28, 1989.

Bernstein, Richard, "The Earnings Surprise Model," *Merrill Lynch Quantitative Viewpoint*, May 22, 1990.

Bernstein, Richard, "Growth & Value," *Merrill Lynch Quantitative Viewpoint*, July 17, 1990.

Bernstein, Richard, "Growth & Value—Part II," *Merrill Lynch Quantititive Viewpoint*, September 25, 1990.

Bernstein, Richard, "Growth & Value—Part III," *Merrill Lynch Quantitative Viewpoint*, October 23, 1991.

Bernstein, Richard, "Growth & Value—Part IV," *Merrill Lynch Quantitative Viewpoint*, June 4, 1991.

Bernstein, Richard, "Yield," *Merrill Lynch Quantitative Viewpoint*, April 7, 1992.

Bernstein, Richard, "Managing Equities Like Bonds, Well Sort of . . ." Presentation to the Institute for International Research Quantitative Investment Management Seminar, October 1992.

Harvey, Campbell R., "Forecasting Economic Growth with the Bond and Stock Markets," *Financial Analysts Journal*, September/October 1989.

Harvey, Campbell R., "Term Structure forecasts Economic Growth," *Financial Analysts Journal*, May/June 1993.

Hagin, Robert L., "The Subtle Risk of High Expected Growth—The Torpedo Effect." Presentation to the Institute for Quantitative Research in Finance, Fall 1991 seminar.

Jacques, William E. and Wood, Arnold S., "Behavioral Justification for the Permanence of the P/E Phenomena." Presentations to the Institute for Quantitative Research in Finance, Fall 1993 seminar.

Peters, Donald J., *A Contrarian Strategy for Growth Stock Investing: Theoretical Foundations & Empirical Evidence.* (Westport, CT: Quorum Books), 1993.

Sharpe, William F., "Asset Allocation: Management Style and Performance Measurement." *Journal of Portfolio Management*. Winter 1992. vol. 18, no. 2. pp. 7–19.

5

High Quality vs. Low Quality

Do "good" companies necessarily make "good" stocks? Intuitively, one would think that they must, but an intriguing question posed by Shefrin and Statman (1993) is whether "good" stocks lead investors to the perception of what is a "good" company. In other words, do investors ferret out "good" companies about which no one knows, or do they see good stock performance and then surmise that it must be because the company is a "good" company? It appears, however, that "bad" companies make better stocks than do "good" companies over the long term. The general tendency nonetheless is to search for "good" companies.

In business schools, they teach that investors need to take more risk in order to get higher returns. Companies that might be superior (or safer) may not be worth investing in because their success has most likely already been discounted into their stock prices. However, investors who followed that advice during the 1980s significantly underperformed investors who were unwilling to take risk. During the 1980s, "good" companies indeed made "good" stocks, and "bad" companies made "bad" stocks. Because of that abnormal risk/return profile (at least by academic standards), by the late 1980s money managers frequently used the adjective high-quality to describe the stocks they picked.

This chapter will define quality, how it has performed historically, how quality-oriented investment returns are affected by

---

the economy, why the 1980s may have been so atypical, and why investors prefer high-quality companies to low-quality ones despite the evidence presented.

Quality, per se, is a relative term. What one considers to be a "good" company at one point in time may be completely different from a "good" company at a different point. In addition, quality may be defined relative to the goals of the particular investment. Guidelines or regulations placed on a certain fund, pension plan, or trust account may restrict quality-oriented strategies so much that the stocks that one manager might consider to be low-quality might be considered very high-quality by another manager.

Investors define quality using any number of different characteristics. Some use debt/equity ratios, and assume that companies without debt are "good" companies, while others use the stability of earnings as a quality guideline. Return on equity, sales growth, earnings growth, and the dispersion of analyst earnings estimates (a measure of disagreement among analysts) are just a few others.

One of the most convenient and informative definitions of quality, but actually one of the least frequently used, is the Standard & Poor's Common Stock Ratings. These ratings are based on the stability and growth in earnings and dividends over a ten-year period (a more full description is published on page 5 of every issue of Standard & Poor's *Stock Guide*). A company with an extremely stable earnings and dividend history would be rated A+, while a company in bankruptcy reorganization would be rated D. S&P calculates these ratings according to a computer algorithm, and there is no subjective analyst interpretation. Thus, although rarely used by investors, S&P has an unbiased quality measure on an extremely large universe of companies.

These ratings are not the better-known S&P Debt Ratings. The debt ratings are based on analyst reviews of company fundamentals regarding the company's ability to repay debt obligations. A study by Healy and Sgromo (1993) suggests that using a quality ranking scheme based on credit ratings probably would not greatly alter the conclusions of the ensuing discussion.

Muller, Fielitz and Greene (1983, 1984) and Muller and Fielitz (1987) appear to have been the first to gauge the information content of these ratings. They found that the S&P Common Stock Ratings were generally a reliable source of company quality, and were actually viable risk proxies. They concluded that A minus-rated stocks were the best performers over the longer term because they were not as overvalued or mispriced as were A+-rated companies, but yet had similar growth-related characteristics. Haugen (1979) came to similar conclusions regarding using common stock ratings as a proxy for risk.

Muller, Fielitz and Greene's conclusions differ from what will be presented here for several reasons. First, their studies did not include B-, C-, or D-rated securities. Second, their universe of stocks was a relatively small 232 companies. Third, they only examined companies whose quality ratings remained unchanged during the fifteen-year period they studied. As we will discuss later, ratings drift, or the changes up or down in a company's S&P rating, may be a source of significant positive or negative returns.

Figure 5.1 shows the distribution of S&P Common Stock Ratings among the roughly 1,500 companies within the Merrill Lynch database (the full S&P universe is larger). One can see that the

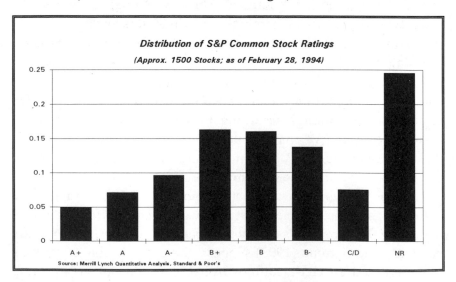

Figure 5.1 Distribution of S&P Common Stock Ratings

distribution of companies is somewhat normal, with very few companies rated A+, and similarly few companies rated C and D. C- and D-rated stocks are grouped together because there are periods during which no stocks were rated D within the 1,500 stock universe.

Note that about 25 percent of the universe has no rating whatsoever. That implies that these companies generally have not been in existence for ten years. The not-rated universe is, therefore, dominated by new issues, and would probably be the universe in which an emerging growth manager might look for investment ideas.

Figures 5.2 to 5.5 show the value of $1 invested on January 31, 1986 in stock portfolios according to S&P Common Stock Ratings. In addition, there are two summary indices: B+ or Better, and B or Worse. The portfolios have been equal-weighted, and were rebalanced monthly. Frequent rebalancing is important because one would want to capture the effect of those low-quality companies that go bankrupt, of companies that outperform as their fundamentals improve prior to their rating being revised upward, and of companies that underperform as their fundamentals deteriorate prior to their rating being downgraded.

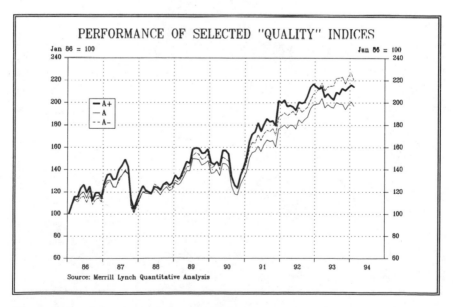

Figure 5.2 A+, A, and A− Stocks

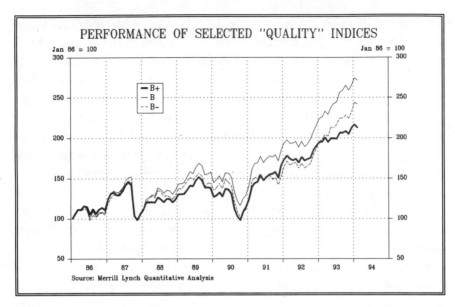

Figure 5.3 B+, B, and B— Stocks

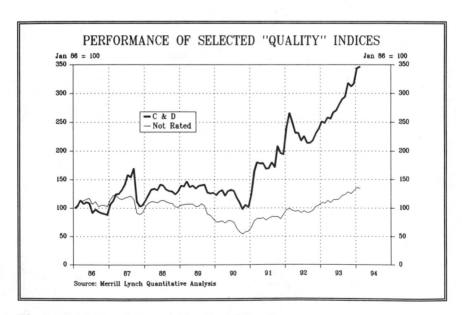

Figure 5.4 C and D and Not Rated Stocks

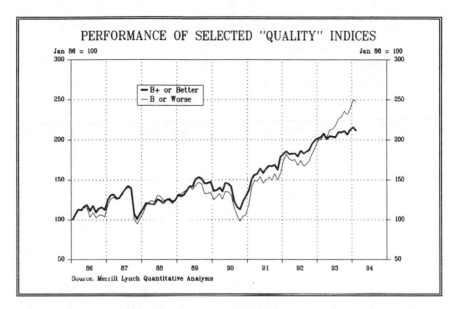

Figure 5.5 B+ or Better Stocks vs. B or Worse Stocks

Altman and Kao (1991, 1992) have done extensive research on what they call ratings drift, or changes in credit quality over time, within corporate bond universes. As one might expect, they found that the ratings of corporate bonds that were highly rated tended to drift downward, while those of noninvestment grade bonds tended to improve. Investment returns related to such drifts moved in similar directions. Although it appears as though no one has studied the effects of ratings drift among common stock ratings, intuitively there is little reason to believe that such studies might yield different results from Altman's and Kao's studies.

Performance related to company quality is often confused with that of cyclical stocks. Some investors assume that all cyclical stocks must necessarily be low-quality stocks, while more stable companies must be higher-quality ones. While it is true that cyclical stocks, by definition, have more variable earnings and, in turn, have lower S&P Common Stock Ratings, higher-quality cyclicals do indeed exist. Similarly, lower-quality stocks do exist within sectors and industries often considered to have stable earnings and dividend histories.

Table 5.1 shows 1993 performance by S&P Common Stock Ratings by economic sector. Figures in bold are the best performing quality segment within each economic sector. One can see that when there is a low-quality effect present within the overall equity market (i.e., stocks rated C and D were up about 33 percent during 1993, while those rated A+ were down about 1.4 percent), it generally does not matter whether one invests in growth stocks, cyclicals, financials, and so on; the quality effect pervades each economic sector.

Another common mistake is to suggest that performance related to quality is a size effect. Size and quality may be intertwined, however, quality-driven markets appear to be so driven across size classifications. Figure 5.6 shows the average market capitalization of the 1,500 stocks grouped by S&P Common Stock Ratings, and size does indeed go down as quality deteriorates. The average A+ company had a market capitalization of approximately $11 billion, while the average C/D company's market capitalization is only about $700 million as of January 31, 1994. However, Table 5.2 shows 1993 performance within size quintiles according to quality ratings. Again, figures in bold represent the best performing quality

Table 5.1 1993 Performance by S&P Common Stock Ratings within Economic Sectors

Sector	A+	A	A−	B+	B	B−	C/D
Credit Cyc	—	12.8	25.9	**29.8**	15.2	10.0	—
Con Gr Stap	−3.9	−6.2	−12.3	4.6	15.2	**24.7**	−15.7
Con Cyc	−2.3	−21.2	36.3	23.0	38.5	**41.7**	9.8
Con Staples	−13.2	−1.8	−0.2	**20.1**	−1.9	−22.2	—
Cap Goods	20.9	−18.8	8.1	5.9	19.5	**33.4**	—
Technology	14.5	16.8	44.8	11.4	**46.9**	31.8	29.1
Energy	—	17.9	15.1	10.3	13.0	**25.1**	−3.2
Basic Inds	−4.5	−13.2	0.2	17.8	30.9	32.8	**37.3**
Financials	−7.0	−4.0	1.5	18.1	21.5	10.8	**28.5**
Transport	—	—	15.3	−1.2	**44.3**	28.4	39.4
Utilities	—	3.1	7.6	7.6	8.4	—	**45.0**

NOTE: Highlighted figures represent the best performing quality group within each economic sector. All performance figures are calculated on an equal-weighted basis.
Source: Merrill Lynch Quantitative Analysis

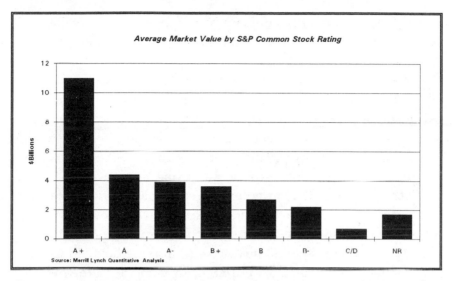

Figure 5.6 Average Company Size by S&P Common Stock Ratings

Table 5.2 1993 Performance by S&P Common Stock Ratings within Size Quintiles

Mkt. Cap.	A+	A	A−	B+	B	B−	C/D
> = 3383M	−4.2	7.1	14.0	16.9	**34.0**	26.9	28.2
1350–3383M	1.4	0.0	0.5	19.3	25.4	32.1	**45.9**
666–1350M	−1.6	−4.6	2.5	13.5	28.1	21.0	**39.9**
255–666M	19.4	2.0	13.6	4.5	17.0	**39.0**	33.6
<255M	−	−6.3	6.0	7.8	12.1	12.0	**20.9**

NOTE: Highlighted figures represent the best performing quality group within each market capitalization quintile. All performance figures are calculated on an equal-weighted basis.
Source: Merrill Lynch Quantitative Analysis

segment. One can see that regardless of whether one was a large capitalization, middle capitalization, or small capitalization investor, it would have been advantageous to have been a lower-quality investor as well. There is no contradiction between Figure 5.6 and Table 5.2. There simply are not the same number of companies found in each cell within the table. An investor interested in large capitalization stocks might find more A+ stocks from which to choose than C or D stocks, and an investor in small capitalization stocks might find more C and D stocks. Regardless of the number of available low-quality companies within one's acceptable universe, it seems as though it would have been preferable to invest in those stocks during 1993.

Although not shown in Figure 5.6 or Table 5.2, the low-quality effect demonstrated here also transgresses categories defined by risk (beta) as well. Regardless of whether one oriented a portfolio toward high-beta or low-beta stocks, it would have been preferable to have invested in low-quality stocks during 1993.

In business schools, one of the prime axioms taught in investment classes is that in order to get higher returns, one must take more risk, and there appears to be some validity to that axiom when one examines the historical returns among quality ratings. That particular concept will be discussed in more detail in Chapter 6 focusing on beta. Table 5.3 examines in more detail the monthly returns that formed the performance charts presented. Return is defined within the table as the average monthly return over the period February 1986 to February 1994. Risk is defined as both the standard deviation (volatility) of the monthly returns, and as the percent of those monthly returns that were negative. While the unpredictability of returns as measured by the standard deviation is the academically preferable method to estimate risk, practitioners often prefer the historical probability of losing money or under-performing a selected benchmark.

**Table 5.3   Risk/Return Characteristics of Quality Indices
Twelve-Month Returns: 1986 to February 1994**

Index	Mean Return	Std. Dev.	% Negative
A+	9.57%	14.83%	23.2%
A	8.83	13.00	24.4
A−	10.59	12.46	20.9
B+	10.43	17.03	27.9
B	13.91	16.71	22.1
B−	12.29	17.48	25.6
C/D	19.28	27.66	25.6
Not Rated	4.01	21.35	43.0

Source: Merrill Lynch Quantitative Analysis

The C/D index does indeed provide the highest twelve-month average return over the time period studied (19.28 percent). However, that additional return is accompanied by significantly more risk. The standard deviation, or predictability, of the C/D index returns is nearly twice as large as those of the A+ and A indices, which implies that one might have more trouble sleeping at night by investing in the C/D index. Standard deviation is discussed in more detail in the Chapter 6. The last column shows risk as defined as the percent of the twelve-month returns that were negative, or a measure of the historical probability of losing money over a twelve-month period. Although the volatility of returns as measured by the standard deviation of the C/D index is substantially higher than that of the higher-quality indices, the percent of the twelve-month returns that were negative is nearly identical across the quality scale. Thus, the C/D index's volatility came from an unpredictable higher positive return. The A+ index historically had negative returns about 23 percent of the time, while the C/D had negative returns 26 percent of the time. Although the likelihood of receiving a negative return was only 3 percent higher for the C/D index, the average return was more than double that of the A+. Thus, "bad" companies have historically made "good" stocks both on an absolute and a risk-adjusted basis.

The relative performance of "bad" companies and "good" companies is not consistent. Historically, "bad" companies have tended to make "good" stocks when the economic and profits cycles improved. It has been the other way around when the economy has contracted. Figures 5.7 and 5.8 show the 1989 and 1990 performance of the universe of stocks included in the study sorted by S&P Common Stock Ratings. Beginning in June 1989, the equity market began to anticipate the upcoming recession. Investors began to look toward "safe havens" for superior returns, and one can see that the quality effect appears to be inverse. That is, "good" companies made "good" stocks.

"Bad" companies have historically not made "good" stocks when the economy slid into recession, because nominal growth rates in profits would decline. It was mentioned before that nominal profits growth is a major determinant of style investment perfor-

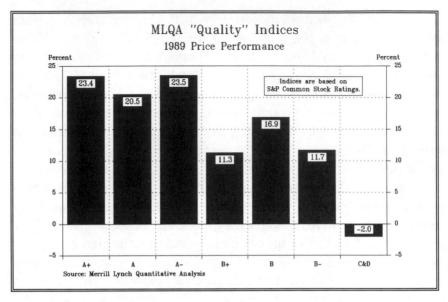

Figure 5.7   1989 Quality Performance

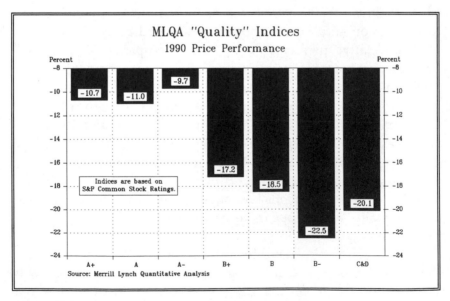

Figure 5.8 · 1990 Quality Performance

mance. As nominal profits growth expanded, regardless of whether that growth was a result of real growth, inflation, or gains in productivity, value investing tended to outperform growth investing. Similarly, when nominal growth rates expand, "bad" companies will make "good" stocks.

That makes sense within the context of the Earnings Expectations Life Cycle. Value investors will tend to reside in the bottom half of the cycle, and most out-of-favor, "bad" companies will also be found in that half. Thus, there may be considerable intertwining between the quality effect and the growth/value effect. Table 5.4 shows the average S&P Common Stock Ratings of the fifty stocks within the S&P 500 with the Lowest Price/Earnings, Price/Book Value, Price/Cash Flow, and Price/Sales ratios during early 1994. The average rating is indeed below that of several growth portfolios. Two of the growth portfolios have atypically low average ratings because of the recent strength in the economy. EPS Momentum and EPS Estimate Revisions have recently shifted toward low-quality stocks because of the earnings strength among more economically sensitive companies.

The correlation between the quality effect and the economy is actually quite extraordinary. The thick line in Figure 5.9 shows the performance of the C/D index relative to that of the A+ index; C/D outperformance is reflected by the periods during which the line rose. The thin line represents the year-to-year percent change in Industrial Production, and is represented on the right scale. Simple correlation analysis suggested that the relative performance of the C/D index has actually forecasted turns in industrial production

Table 5.4 Average S&P Stock Ratings of Selected Value and Growth Portfolios—February 1994

Value Portfolios	Avg. Rating	Growth Portfolios	Avg. Rating
Low P/E	B+	High Proj. Growth	A−
Low P/B	B	EPS Surprise	A−
Low P/CF	B+	EPS Est. Revision	B
Low P/S	B	EPS Momentum	B

Source: Merrill Lynch Quantitative Analysis

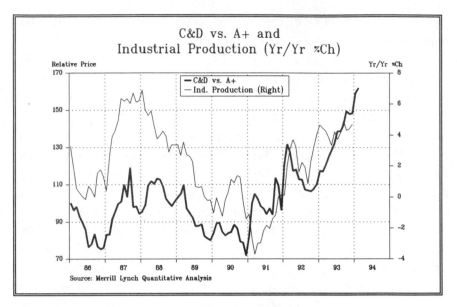

Figure 5.9 C/D vs. A+ and Industrial Production

over the last five or six years by, on average, about six months. Thus, not only is the relative performance of lower-quality stocks dependent on the economy, but it actually appears to be a worthwhile economic forecasting tool as well.

The risk of bankruptcy is an important consideration when investing in low-quality stocks. After all, a company rated D is already in bankruptcy reorganization. As the economy and nominal growth rates expand, the risk of bankruptcy probably declines. If the economy is doing well, and the general business climate is encouraging, it is simply harder for a company to go bankrupt.

Companies that have higher fixed costs, as opposed to variable costs, have a higher bankruptcy potential as the economy moves from expansion to recession. High fixed costs are usually the result of predetermined obligations. For example, fixed costs can be the result of debt issuance or necessary capital stock and its related leases in order to operate. Fixed costs cannot be decreased as the business cycle turns down; debt must be repaid and capital equipment is still needed to operate. The airline industry is notorious for having high fixed costs because much of their financing is lease-

or debt-related, and the cost of operating a plane is roughly the same whether the plane is full or has one passenger aboard. Labor, by contrast, is a variable cost. If the business environment turns bad, the manager can lay off workers in order to lower the cost structure of the company.

Lower-quality companies tend to have higher fixed costs. For example, Figure 5.10 shows the average debt/total capitalization ratio of the stocks within the universe cited sorted by S&P Common Stock Ratings. One can see that debt/total capitalization ratios tend to go up, implying higher fixed costs, as the quality rating goes down.

Higher fixed costs, such as debt, make lower-quality companies more economically sensitive, and more dependent on nominal growth rates to improve. That effect is evident in Figure 5.11, which compares the relative performances (versus the equal-weighted S&P 500) of the fifty stocks within the S&P Industrials with the highest debt/equity ratios and those with the lowest debt/equity ratios. When the line rises, the particular strategy is outperforming the overall market, and underperforming when it falls. From 1989 to 1991, investors were quite concerned about a potential recession and its lingering effects, and the high debt/equity portfolios con-

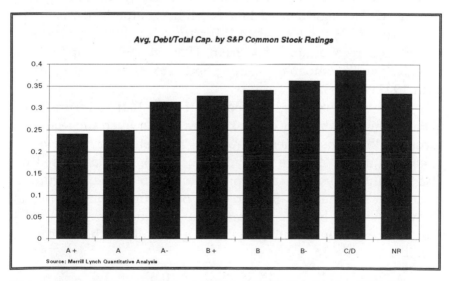

Figure 5.10 Debt as a Percent of Total Capitalization by S&P Common Stock Ratings

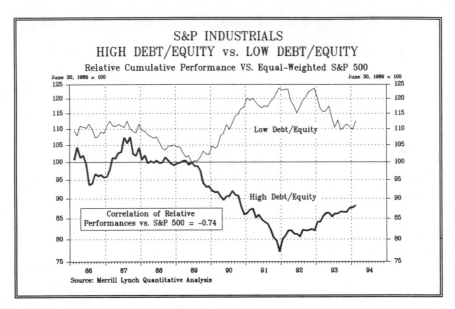

Figure 5.11 High Debt/Equity vs. Low Debt/Equity

siderably underperformed the overall market. Investors preferred low debt/equity stocks that were viewed as having a lower probability of failing during the recession because of their lower cost structures. The high debt/equity portfolios outperformed significantly from 1991 to 1993 when it became clear that the economy was indeed recovering. Thus, from 1989 to 1991, it appears as though "good" companies made "good" stocks, but that reversed from 1991 to 1993.

Bernstein (1989) highlighted that stocks that were predicted to have a high probability of bankruptcy but survived subsequently substantially outperformed the overall market. That report highlighted Altman's Z-Score (see Altman, 1983), a model based on discriminant analysis that attempts to predict corporate bankruptcy. Companies that had a Z-Score of 1.81 or less in Altman's original study showed a higher propensity to eventually declare bankruptcy. The formula relating to that 1.81 cutoff for the Z-Score is as follows:

$$Z = 1.2X_1 + 1.4X_2 + 3.3X_3 + 0.6X_4 + 1.0X_5$$

where,

X_1 = working capital/total assets,

X_2 = retained earnings (balance sheet)/total assets,

X_3 = EBIT/total assets,

X_4 = market value of all equity/total liabilities,

X_5 = sales/total assets.

The Z-Score is a combination of a debt/equity ratio (actually an equity/debt ratio) and a series of asset turnover ratios. Companies that have high debt levels and do not use their assets efficiently are more prone to bankruptcy than would be those with little debt and efficient asset utilization. Companies with lower fixed costs can still go bankrupt, according to the model, if they are extremely inefficient users of their assets.

All companies that the Z-Score model highlighted as being bankruptcy candidates did not necessarily go bankrupt, and the stocks of those companies that survived tended to outperform the overall equity market handily. Bernstein's sample had an imbedded survivorship bias (bankrupt companies were removed from the sample's history), and he found that companies with extremely low Z-Scores that did not declare bankruptcy actually outperformed both the overall market, and those companies with high Z-Scores. He concluded that the results suggested that those willing to accept the additional risk of turnaround situations might be rewarded for finding those companies that survive.

If "bad" companies make "good" stocks, then why were investor perceptions regarding that relative performance so reversed during the 1980s? The profits and economic cycles were extremely anemic during the late 1980s. As was pointed out earlier, the longest profits recession of the entire post-war period took place during those years. In addition, inflation was washed out of the U.S. economy during the decade, and caused two problems for the traditional risk/return relationship. First, without inflation, a major source of nominal growth was lost, and companies (often the poorer-quality ones) that relied on price increases to grow profits could no longer do so. Second, more stable companies that could not pass along inflationary pressures to their customers saw profits margins expand as their costs stabilized. Thus, stable "good" companies benefited from the disinflation and deflation, while more economically sensitive "bad" companies lost a major source of profits growth. Over the past couple of years, productivity has replaced inflation as a major contributor to nominal growth, and "bad" companies have begun to again outperform.

Table 5.5 shows real gross domestic product, inflation, and productivity by five-year periods. Overall nominal growth, here simply implied as the sum of real GDP and inflation as measured by the Consumer Price Index, was indeed extremely weak during the second half of the 1980s and early 1990s.

Despite the evidence, institutional investors still generally tend to search for "good" companies rather than for "good" stocks. There may be several factors that might contribute to that tendency, such as a lack of available research, lack of trading liquidity, and psychological barriers.

There has been considerable academic literature on what has come to be known as the *neglected* stock effect. Perhaps the most famous articles are those by Arbel, Carvell, and Strebel (1983) and by Arbel and Strebel (1982, 1983). In those articles, the authors point out that information is not uniformly available for all stocks. For large well-known stocks, there is considerable information available nearly daily. However, for smaller, lesser-known companies information may be sporadic at best. That information asymmetry may be an opportunity for those investors willing to do their

Table 5.5 Historical Economic Indicators

Time Period	Real GDP	CPI	Productivity
60–64	5.0%	1.3%	4.8%
65–69	4.2	3.4	6.2
70–74	2.5	6.1	2.9
75–79	3.2	8.5	3.6
80–84	1.8	7.8	1.7
85–89	3.1	3.6	2.7
90–93	1.2	3.9	1.2

Source: Merrill Lynch Economics

own research on the ignored or neglected companies. They believed that the information asymmetry was a flaw in the efficient market hypothesis because there simply was no means for information relating to certain stocks to flow quickly through the financial markets and be immediately discounted.

Table 5.6 shows that the quality effect may be influenced by the neglected stock effect. The table shows the average number of analysts among companies grouped by S&P Common Stock Ratings. The average A+ company has more than twenty analysts following the stock, while only about two analysts tend to follow the average D stock. One should find it perplexing that so many analysts follow A+ companies and so few follow Ds. A+ companies are those with the most stable earnings and dividend patterns; what is there to analyze? The analyst can simply extrapolate trend. However, few analysts research the companies for which only one question must be answered: Will the company survive? It is often a very difficult question, but a correct answer may give insight as to whether one should buy or short the particular stock, and may yield tremendous returns.

Of course, the analyst who follows the A+ company has plenty to analyze regarding whether one should indeed extrapolate

Table 5.6 Analyst Coverage by S&P Common Stock Ratings—February 1994

S&P Common Stock Ratings	Approx. Average Number of Research Analysts
A+	21
A	16
A−	16
B+	13
B	12
B−	9
C	7
D	2
NR	8

Source: Merrill Lynch Quantitative Analysis

the trendline in earnings and dividends, or should one be wary of some upcoming torpedo. Within the context of the Earnings Expectations Life Cycle, enthusiasm for a stock comes right at the stock's performance and expectations peak. Thus, most analysts believe that the "good" company's good fortunes will undoubtedly continue, and they simply extrapolate trend. The investor is left to ultimately wonder what happened to the performance of the so-called "good" company.

Analyst extrapolation of trend for "good" companies and the lack of research coverage for "bad" companies may be a factor that contributes to stock price overreaction. DeBondt and Thaler (1986) and Chopra, Lakonishok, and Ritter (1992), among others, have discussed how stock prices tend to overreact to company news. They both find that perceived losers tend to outperform perceived winners after a news event, and that outperformance related to an overreaction can last for several years.

Institutional investors tend to invest in stocks that have adequate trading liquidity. Trading liquidity refers to the amount of a stock that trades for a given period of time, and is important to institutional investors because it allows them to gauge how large a position they can take in a stock and, in some cases, how quickly they can get out of a position should something go wrong. Table 5.7 shows a simple measure of trading liquidity and trading volume, across quality ratings, and demonstrates another potential reason why some investors gravitate toward high-quality issues. It is rather ironic that the need to *escape* from a stock position would decrease if one simply searched for "good" stocks instead of "good" companies.

Shefrin and Statman (1993) suggest another reason that investors tend to shun low-quality companies. They suggest that portfolio managers are more regret-averse than they are risk-averse. Regret-aversion is based on cognitive psychology, and suggests that portfolio managers orient portfolios so they will not have to apologize to their clients. They feel that if a manager buys the stock of a "good" company, and the stock subsequently underperforms, then the manager can claim that it was not his or her fault. After all, the company was indeed a well-known "good" company, but

Table 5.7   Trading Volume by S&P Common Stock Ratings— February 1994

S&P Common Stock Ratings	Avg. Weekly Trading Volume During Prior 52 Weeks (000's)
A+	2284
A	1099
A−	1017
B+	1121
B	1373
B−	1310
C	1123
D	875
NR	931

Source: Merrill Lynch Quantitative Analysis

that some outside influence altered the investment returns from those that were expected. For example, management might have made bad decisions or the market simply favored low-quality companies. However, if the manager buys a well-known "bad" company, and it subsequently underperforms, then the risk of being fired goes up for the manager. It may appear to the client that everyone in the world knew that the company was a "bad" company except this one idiotic manager. Thus, managers never want to face regret, and tend to manage their portfolios accordingly.

This chapter has tried to demonstrate that although one might have to sometimes confront regret, the returns to investing in "bad" companies have historically not only compensated for their risks, but also for their regrets. That statement is more difficult to justify for "good" companies.

◆ Summary

- ◆ Contrary to popular belief, "good" companies do not necessarily make "good" stocks. More often than not, it is "bad" companies that make "good" stocks.

♦ An easy and readily available means for measuring quality is the Standard & Poor's Common Stock Ratings. These ratings are based on the stability and growth in earnings and dividends over a ten-year period.

♦ An index of C- and D-rated companies significantly outperformed those rated A+ over the time period studied. That performance remained superior even on a risk-adjusted basis.

♦ The profits cycle has a direct impact on whether "bad" companies make "good" stocks. "Good" companies do indeed make "good" stocks when profits growth declines. However, because the U.S. economy is a growth-oriented economy, and the economy spends more time in expansion than recession, a relatively small number of firms go bankrupt, and "bad" companies tend to make "good" stocks through time.

♦ Lower-quality companies tend to have higher fixed costs, such as debt. Those higher fixed costs lead to potential bankruptcy, and lead investors to invest in safe havens during times of poor profitability.

♦ Altman's Z-Scores, a predictor of bankruptcy, were used as another measure of quality. Companies with low Z-Scores, or a high probability of bankruptcy, that do not declare bankruptcy have historically outperformed the overall market.

♦ Despite considerable research suggesting that one should search for "good" stocks, institutional investors tend to search for "good" companies. Factors such as a lack of available research information, trading liquidity, and psychological factors may influence the investment process and lead toward searching for "good" companies.

♦ Neglected stocks are those for which there is little or no research coverage, and it has been shown that such stocks tend to outperform the overall market. There is an abundance of research regarding "good" companies, but very little regarding "bad" companies.

♦ Regret-aversion may better describe how some portfolios are managed than does the traditional risk-aversion. The fear of regret may be a significant psychological factor that leads portfolio managers toward "good" companies.

◆ *References*

Altman, Edward I., *Corporate Financial Distress* (New York: John Wiley & Sons, Inc.), 1983.

Altman, Edward I., and Duen Li Kao, "Corporate Bond Rating Drift: An Examination of Rating Agency Credit Quality Changes" (Charlottesville, VA: Association for Investment Management Research), 1991.

Altman, Edward I., and Duen Li Kao, "Rating Drift in High Yield Bonds," *The Journal of Fixed Income*, March 1992.

Arbel, Avner and Strebel, Paul, "The Neglected and Small Firm Effects," *Financial Review*, 1982, vol. 17, no. 4, pp. 201–218.

Arbel, Avner, Carvell, Steven, and Strebel, Paul, "Giraffes, Institutions and Neglected Firms," *Financial Analysts Journal*, 1983, vol. 39, no. 3, pp. 57–63.

Bernstein, Richard, "The Decaying *Financial* Infrastructure," *Merrill Lynch Quantitative Viewpoint*, June 6, 1989.

Bernstein, Richard and Pradhuman, Satya, "A 'Low Quality' Market," *Merrill Lynch Quantitative Viewpoint*, January 12, 1993.

Bernstein, Richard and Pradhuman, Satya, "Introducing the MLQA 'Quality' Indices," *Merrill Lynch Quantitative Viewpoint*, March 23, 1993.

Bernstein, Richard and Pradhuman, Satya, "It's Not Small, It's Not Cyclical, It's 'Low Quality'," *Merrill Lynch Quantitative Viewpoint*, August 24, 1993.

Bernstein, Richard and Pradhuman, Satya, "Quality Review & Preview," *Merrill Lynch Quantitative Viewpoint*, January 11, 1994.

Bernstein, Richard and Pradhuman, Satya, "Value Managers: It May Be Too Early To Invest For Recession," *Merrill Lynch Quantitative Viewpoint*, February 22, 1994.

Chopra, Navin, Lakonishok, Josef, and Ritter, Jay R., "Measuring Abnormal Performance: Do Stocks Overreact?" *Journal of Financial Economics*, 1992, vol. 31, pp. 235–268.

DeBondt, Werner F. M. and Thaler, Richard H., "Does the Stock Market Overreact?" *Journal of Finance*, July 1986, vol. XL, no. 3, pp. 793–807.

Healy, C. Ross and Sgromo, Enrico, "How to Beat the S&P 500 Index Using Credit Analysis Alone," *Journal of Portfolio Management*, Winter 1993, pp. 25–31.

Muller, Frederick L. and Fielitz, Bruce D., "Standard & Poor's Quality Rankings Revisited," *Journal of Portfolio Management*, Spring 1987, pp. 64–68.

Muller, Frederick L., Fielitz, Bruce D., and Green, Myron T. "S&P Quality Group Rankings: Risk and Return," *Journal of Portfolio Management*, Summer 1983, pp. 39–42.

Muller, Frederick L., Fielitz, Bruce D., and Greene, Myron T., "Portfolio Performance in Relation to Quality, Earnings, Dividends, Firm Size, Leverage, and Return on Equity," *Journal of Financial Research*, 1984, vol. 7, no. 1, pp. 17–26.

Shefrin, Hersh and Statman, Meir, "A Behavioral Framework for Expected Stock Returns," Santa Clara University working paper, October 1993.

Strebel, Paul J. and Arbel, Avner, "Pay Attention to Neglected Firms!" *Journal of Portfolio Management*, 1983, vol. 9, no. 2, pp. 37–42.

Thaler, Richard H., *Advances in Behavioral Finance* (New York: Russell Sage Foundation), 1993.

6

High Beta vs. Low Beta

◆

*B*eta is a traditional measure of risk that originated within the efficient market writings of Sharpe (1970, for example). More recently, much of the financial literature has questioned beta's viability as a risk measure because, contrary to theory, lower beta stocks outperformed higher beta stocks during much of the 1980s. "Is beta dead?" and "Why should investors bother to take risk when lower beta stocks outperform higher beta stocks?" have been frequently asked. In this chapter, we will define beta, discuss why it did not work during the 1980s, whether it will once again work as a viable risk measure, and that its purported death seems to have been somewhat premature.

Figure 6.1 shows the performance of the fifty stocks in the S&P 500 with the highest betas relative to that of the equal-weighted S&P 500. The high beta portfolio has been rebalanced monthly, and stocks are held in equal weights. The high beta portfolio significantly underperformed the overall equity market during the second half of the 1980s (the relative performance line goes down). The efficient market hypothesis suggests that higher beta stocks should outperform in order to compensate investors for the added risk of those stocks, but one can see that did not happen during much of the 1980s. The reaction to that apparent contradiction to the efficient market hypothesis was a stream of financial articles written by both academics and practitioners regarding the

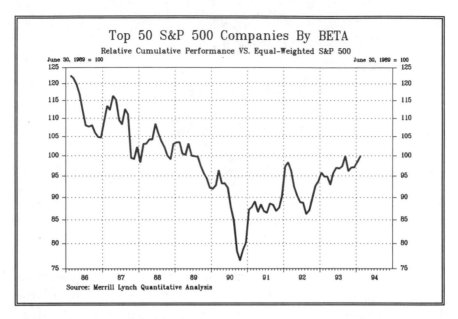

Figure 6.1   Top 50 Stocks by Beta

demise of beta. Recent articles include those of Fama and French (1992) and Grinold (1993).

As this book has tried to point out, when a strong consensus forms regarding nearly anything in the financial markets, the consensus is usually proved to be incorrect. Note that the high-beta portfolio has significantly outperformed the overall market since November 1990. So, just when everyone was searching for new risk/return relationships, beta seems once again to be doing a pretty good job.

Traditional financial research assumes that risk is a predictor of return because investors must be compensated for taking risk. Throughout this chapter, one should keep an important question in mind: Was beta a poor predictor of risk during the 1980s, or was it a good predictor of risk, but investors simply were aware that they were not being compensated for taking risk and, therefore, invested in low beta stocks? Academic literature assumes a "rational" investor. Investors might have been quite rational during the 1980s, and found superior risk/return relationships among lower beta stocks. Those less risky and superior returns continued until investors overwhelmingly realized the superior risk/return potential offered by lower beta stocks. Eventually, so many investors attempted to grab on to those low risk returns that the relative advantage to low beta investing was arbitraged away. That is exactly what should have happened according to the efficient market hypothesis, but it appears to have taken five to ten years for that arbitrage to take place.

Beta measures a stock's risk within the context of a well-diversified portfolio, but it is often confused with the risk of a particular stock held alone. Academic studies have traditionally defined a stock's risk in terms of the variability of its returns. In other words, if a stock always returned 5 percent a year, then investing in the stock would carry little risk because the investor expected a 5 percent return with near certainty. On the other hand, another stock might average 5 percent return a year, but that return might vary between 0 percent and 10 percent. An investor might expect the 5 percent average return, but it was likely that the true returns might never be 5 percent. Thus, using the traditional definition of risk, the second stock would be riskier than the first. In fact, one would have to wonder why anyone would hold the second stock, when the first stock offered the same return through time, and would have allowed one to sleep better at night.

Figure 6.2 shows the relationship between two such stocks. The horizontal axis on the graph depicts the risk of the two stocks as measured by their variability in returns. Stocks to the left have more predictable/less variable returns than do those to the right. The vertical axis measures their average annual return. The first stock (A) sits directly to the left of the second (B) because they have the same annual average return, but A's return is more certain. The goal within this type of chart is to invest in securities that are as far northwest within the chart as possible. In other words, one would like to find the highest returns possible (north) with the less risk (west). Although A does not sit northwest of B, it does sit directly west, and thus is preferable. Similarly, stocks that lie directly north of others are preferable because they offer higher return at identical risk levels. In the chart, (C) would be preferable to (B).

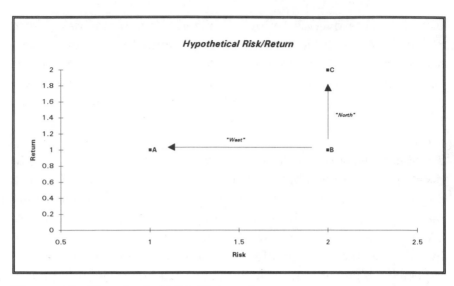

Figure 6.2   Hypothetical Risk/Return Space

In Figure 6.2 the firm's total risk is measured by the standard deviation of returns. Standard deviation is a statistical measure of variability; in finance, larger standard deviations suggest that returns are less predictable. In the first example, one stock has a standard deviation of 0; its returns never vary, while the second stock standard deviation is larger by definition because its returns vary between 0 percent and 10 percent. The standard deviation is considered to measure the total risk of a company because it measures the total volatility of its stock returns.

The volatility or total risk can be broken down into two components: *firm-specific risk* and *nondiversifiable risk*. Firm-specific risk is the risk or volatility attributable only to circumstances regarding the particular company. That risk can be the result of, for example, the chairman dying, of changes in government regulation, or of being awarded a new contract. A new customer contract does not affect all the stocks within the equity market, but rather only the particular company. If the contract were won, then it might affect the firm's competitors and suppliers as events particular to those firms. Within the context of a well-diversified portfolio, such risk can be negated or canceled by the firm-specific risk of other stocks.

Investors' reactions affecting the stock of the company that won the contract might be offset by the reaction in the stock of the company that lost it. Firm-specific risk tends to be reduced as the number of stocks within the portfolio rises because the odds of firm-specific risks counterbalancing each other go up. Eventually, increasing the number of stocks held within the portfolio will eliminate all firm-specific risk, and the portfolio characteristics will resemble those of the overall equity market. A one-stock portfolio, therefore, is totally subject to firm-specific risk, but the overall market may be virtually immune. Thus, firm-specific risk is often referred to as *diversifiable risk.*

Beta, however, is a measure of a firm's nondiversifiable risk or that risk which remains after sufficient diversification. Another name for beta is *market-related risk.* If the market goes up, the efficient markets hypothesis states, then the odds are that a portfolio of stocks will go up as well no matter how well diversified that portfolio might be. If the market goes down, then the portfolio would tend to go down. Beta is a linear measure of that relationship, and a portfolio with a beta of 1.50 would tend to rise or fall 15 percent for every 10 percent move for the S&P 500.

Investors often confuse beta with standard deviation, and nondiversifiable risk with diversifiable risk. Beta is a stock's risk solely within the context of a well-diversified portfolio, while standard deviation is the stock's total risk or overall volatility. An investor who has a one-stock portfolio of a high beta stock should not be surprised when the stock's performance does not seem to adhere to the linear relationship implied by its beta. The firm-specific risk could be a very large proportion of the stock's total risk.

Beta is formally defined within the Capital Pricing Model (CAPM), and is considered to be the linear relationship between a particular stock's returns and those of the overall market. The market is usually represented by the S&P 500, although, some measures incorporate the NYSE or some other universe as a benchmark. The returns used are traditionally five years of monthly total returns, but some betas are calculated using shorter time periods and/or weekly instead of monthly returns. Five years has been the traditional time period because it was thought that five years would generally encompass a full market or economic cycle.

Betas are usually calculated according to the CAPM using linear regression according to the following simple equation. One will note that, by definition, the market has a beta of 1.00.

$$RETURN_{STOCK} = a + \beta RETURN_{MARKET} + e,$$

where,

α = the alpha intercept or average performance above what could be explained by beta,

β = the beta or regression coefficient measuring the linear relationship between market and stock returns, and

e = an unexplained error term.

This is the simplest form of beta. More sophisticated betas include those that are adjusted to be more forward looking or predictive of future betas, those that are based on more factors than the market alone, and those that are based on accounting statistics. For the purpose of this book, the simple definition will suffice, although there has been considerable academic and professional discussion as to whether that simple definition is indeed the correct one.

The error term, e, represents the firm-specific risk. Some stock's values for e would be positive and some negative, and individual values for e would tend to cancel each other out within a diversified portfolio. Portfolio returns are, therefore, a function purely of alpha and beta but individual stock returns are a function of alpha, beta, and e. A portfolio with a positive alpha suggests that the manager of the portfolio may have had some stock selection skill because the portfolio returns were above what could be explained by beta and attributable to the market risk of the portfolio. If the alpha is negative, then it suggests that the manager's stock selection may have detracted from portfolio performance. Figure 6.3 depicts a hypothetical manager with a positive alpha, and one with a negative alpha. If all alphas were 0, then the portfolios would depict the linear relationship implied by beta. Those that are above the line have positive alphas and have been more

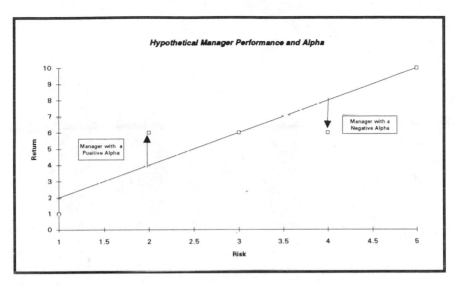

Figure 6.3 Hypothetical Manager Alpha

than compensated for the risk within the portfolio implied by beta. In those cases, the manager has been able to uncover undervalued stocks. Those portfolios that are below the line have negative alphas, and have not been compensated for their imbedded beta risk. In those cases, the manager has probably been buying overvalued stocks.

There are many factors that can contribute to a company's volatility of returns and, in turn, to its beta. Dividend yield, leverage, asset volatility, and market value, to name a few, can help determine the company's ultimate beta. The following figures compare the betas of an approximate 1,000-stock universe when those companies are divided into quintiles according to various characteristics as of December 31, 1993.

Figure 6.4 compares the betas of the quintiles sorted by size. Larger stocks tend to have lower betas than do smaller stocks. The higher nondiversifiable risk of smaller stocks may be related to their increased economic sensitivity. That topic will be discussed in more detail in Chapter 8, but for now it will suffice to say that smaller stocks are extremely economically sensitive, and as such may respond more vigorously to economic upturns and downturns than does the overall market.

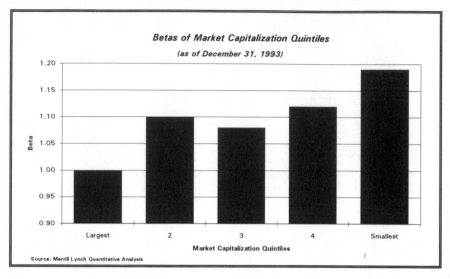

Figure 6.4   Beta by Market Capitalization Quintiles

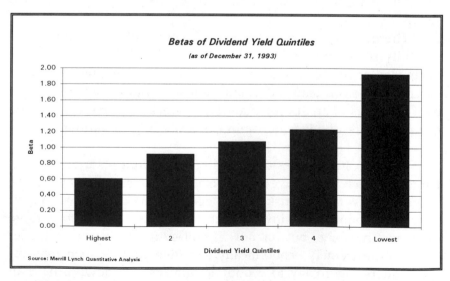

Figure 6.5   Beta by Dividend Yield Quintiles

Figure 6.5 examines beta by quintiles of dividend yield, and higher yielding stocks tend to have lower betas. There are several reasons why stocks with higher yields tend to have lower betas. One reason is that cash is a zero-beta asset. In other words, cash holds its value (in nominal terms) regardless of the performance of the equity market, and has always been the proverbial "stuff it in a mattress" asset. In essence, a dividend is a cash payment made to the investor by the issuing company. Although one cannot be guaranteed that the payment will be made, the dividend portion of a stock's total return is relatively certain compared to potential capital appreciation. Obviously, companies increase, decrease, or even omit their dividends, but dividends in aggregate are relatively certain. Because cash is a zero-beta asset, stocks whose total return is comprised of a larger proportion of dividends will tend to have lower betas, similar to the beta of a two-asset portfolio comprised of one zero-beta asset and one stock.

One theory of dividend payout is that companies that pay higher dividends do so because they tend to have fewer growth opportunities (see Miller and Modigliani (1961), Gordon (1963), and Baskin (1989)). A corporation can seek to enhance shareholder value either by paying out profits to the shareholder in the form of dividends or by reinvesting profits into some venture or capital project that the firm feels will have a higher return on investment than that otherwise available to the shareholder. By not paying out profits in the form of dividends, however, the corporation implicitly assumes that it is a better investment or asset manager than is the individual shareholder, and makes a judgment that investing in a "portfolio" of the corporate assets will provide superior returns to that of the overall market. Thus, companies with greater growth prospects tend to have higher betas because the assets in which investments are made are not as diverse as those of all the companies in the full market. The certainty of return decreases because of that lack of diversification, and as that certainty decreases, the beta will rise. Both the total risk and nondiversifiable risk of such companies will be higher.

Figure 6.6 shows betas by growth sector classification. Defensive stocks are those that tend to pay higher dividends and have fewer growth opportunities, while growth stocks are those that pay lower dividends or do not pay dividends at all, and assume that their return on investment or return on assets will be superior to that of the overall market.

Beta appears to be slightly more related to potential growth than to value. Table 6.1 shows the five-year projected earnings growth rate and the price/earnings and price/book value ratios for beta quintiles as of December 31, 1993. It appears as though five-year projected growth rates increase as beta increases, but that the valuation ratios do not deviate substantially from each other. Low-

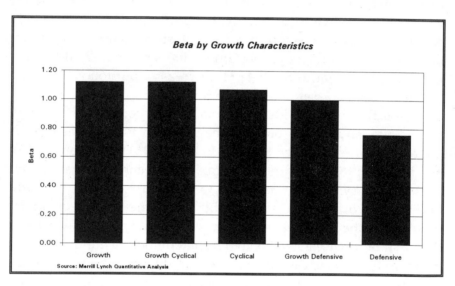

Figure 6.6 Beta by Growth Characteristics

Table 6.1 Growth and Value by Beta Quintile in 1993

Beta Quintile	Proj. 5 Yr. EPS Gr.	P/E	P/B
Lowest	10.0	16.8	3.9
2	10.5	18.7	3.6
3	14.3	19.0	4.9
4	13.9	19.2	4.3
Highest	14.8	18.7	4.2

Source: Merrill Lynch Quantitative Analysis

est beta stocks do have lower five-year projected earnings growth rates and lower P/E ratios, but their price/book value ratios appear roughly similar to those of the other quintiles. Quintile 2 does have a lower growth rate, but its valuations are nearly identical to those of the higher beta quintiles.

Although one might argue that 1993 may not be a representative year, data from other years seems to support the contention. Table 6.2 is based on data from December 1983, and yields somewhat similar conclusions. P/E ratios, in general, were substantially lower in 1983 than they were in 1993 because of the inverse impacts that inflation and disinflation and rising and falling interest rates have on valuation levels. Price/Book Value ratios were not available for 1983 within the Merrill Lynch database.

Figure 6.7 examines betas by interest rate sensitivity. The concept of duration was discussed briefly in Chapter 4 on growth and value, and will be discussed further in Chapter 7. Duration is a measure of interest rate sensitivity, and longer duration bonds and stocks tend to be more interest rate sensitive than are those of shorter durations. The market itself is interest rate sensitive, and as interest rates change, the stock market reacts accordingly. It follows that longer duration or more interest rate sensitive stocks tend to have higher betas than do shorter duration, less interest rate sensitive stocks.

We mentioned the importance of earnings expectations and how one could conceivably obtain higher returns if one had superior fundamental research and could forecast earnings surprises. Beta actually appears to have no relationship with earnings sur-

Table 6.2   **Growth and Value by Beta Quintile in 1983**

Beta Quintile	Proj. 5 Yr Gr.	P/E
Lowest	9.5	8.3
2	15.4	10.0
3	12.8	9.8
4	14.0	10.0
Highest	17.9	12.2

Source: Merrill Lynch Quantitative Analysis

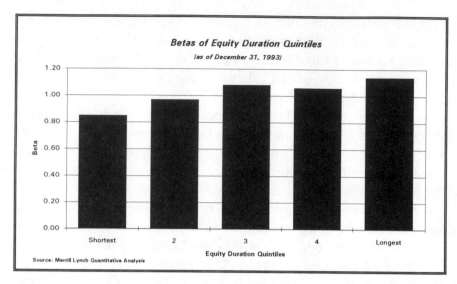

Figure 6.7   Beta by Equity Duration

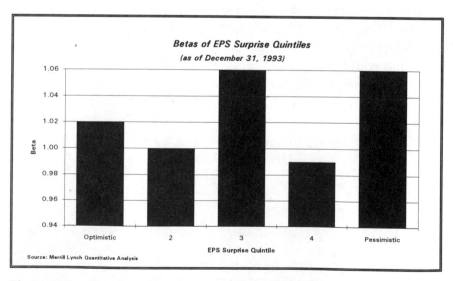

Figure 6.8   Beta by Earnings Surprise Candidates

prises. Figure 6.8 shows the relationship between stocks in the Merrill Lynch Quantitative Analysis Earnings Surprise Model and beta as of year-end 1993. The betas show no particular pattern among either potential positive or negative surprise candidates.

Chapter 5 dealt with company quality, and it was stated that performance related to S&P Common Stock Ratings was not attributable to beta. It was shown that low quality outperformed high quality during 1993 regardless of the constraint one placed on beta. However, if one turns that relationship around, and controls for quality instead of for beta, one finds the average beta for each quality rating quite different. As Figure 6.9 demonstrates, lower-quality companies tend to have higher betas. Lower-quality companies tend not to pay dividends because their cash flows do not permit it. The average dividend yield among companies rated C and D is roughly 0. Thus, low-quality companies have higher betas for the reasons mentioned, except they do not plow back profits into their businesses at a high rate. They have higher betas purely because their return streams are so unstable.

This topic will be discussed in more detail in Chapter 8 on small stock investing. A differentiation will be made between

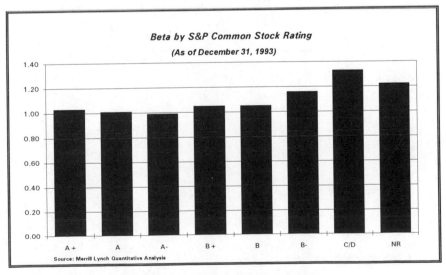

Figure 6.9 Beta by S&P Common Stock Rating

emerging growth stocks that plow back nearly all their profits, and small capitalization value stocks, which are small companies that used to be larger, and may have cut or omitted their dividends during the unwanted metamorphosis from large to small.

Traditional finance suggests that investors who structure higher beta portfolios should be compensated for taking that extra risk and, therefore, the line represented by the equation described earlier, often called the Security Market Line, should always be upward sloping. An upward slope would indicate that investors were being compensated for additional risk because higher betas would be associated with higher expected returns. During the 1980s, that relationship seems to have deteriorated, and at times the Security Market Line was flat to downward sloping. A flat line suggests that expected returns are identical across the entire risk spectrum. If that were the case, then the rational investor would surely hold the riskless asset, for one could get identical returns regardless of whether one took risk or not. Investors would simply shift westward in risk/return space.

Figures 6.10 and 6.11, which follow, compare the Security Market Lines from December 1983 with that from December 1993

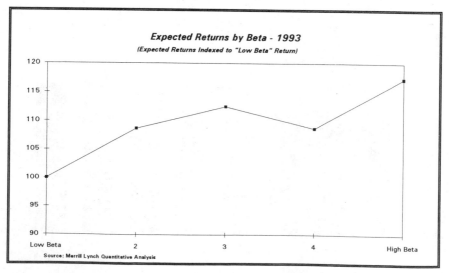

Figure 6.10 The Security Market Line in 1993

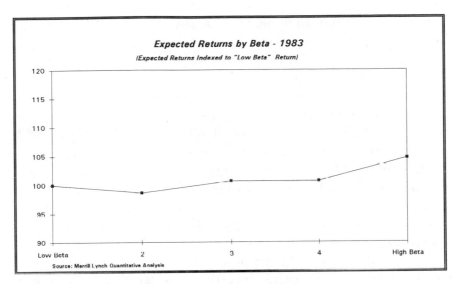

Figure 6.11   The Security Market Line in 1983

by examining expected returns by beta quintiles. Betas are calculated based on sixty months of price returns for the individual security versus those for the S&P 500. They are then adjusted using a method similar to that suggested by Blume (1975) to be more forward-looking or predictive, and are grouped into fifths according to the number of companies within the universe at a given point in time. Expected returns are from the Merrill Lynch Quantitative Analysis Dividend Discount Model which presently estimates expected returns on about six hundred companies.

Although the data suggest that the Security Market Line was not downward sloping in 1983, it is certainly less steep than the 1993 line. The security market lines have been indexed so that the lowest beta quintile equals 100 because all expected returns were substantially higher in 1983 than in 1993 due to the impact that inflation had on analyst estimates in 1983 and that disinflation had on estimates in 1993. By indexing the two beta ranges, one can easily see the different slopes or risk/return tradeoffs.

During much of the 1980s, there may have been little or no incentive to take risk. Superior, or at least competitive, returns were available among lower beta, safer stocks, and investors saw no extra advantage to taking additional risk. A steeper Security Market Line might entice investors to take additional risk, but the line was so flat during much of the 1980s that investors generally saw no incremental benefit to risk-taking.

As Table 6.3 demonstrates, lower beta stocks often outperformed higher beta stocks during the past nine years, contrary to what theory would have suggested. Chan and Lakonishok (1993) have pointed out that although their findings suggest that beta is not a terrific predictor of returns, it was an atypically poor predictor during the 1980s. Beta's predictive abilities appear to be strong if one ends a study prior to 1980, but weaken when one includes the 1980s. In retrospect, it is clear that the security market line was not steep enough to entice investors to take risk.

The efficient market hypothesis implies that an opportunity to get superior returns while incurring less risk should be quickly arbitraged away. However, that theory suggests that all investors perceive a risk/return opportunity the same way, and the Earnings Expectations Life Cycle indicates that universal acceptance of investment ideas is rare, and that investors have the tendency to both positively and negatively overreact. If all investors had the same perceptions of investment opportunities, then the arbitrage suggested by the efficient markets hypothesis should occur quickly. In reality, the annual performance table shows that the arbitrage seems to have taken five to ten years to complete.

Table 6.3   Annual Performance: High vs. Low Beta Stocks

	High Beta Portfolio	Low Beta Portfolio
1985	12.7	13.6
1986	5.3	6.7
1987	16.1	1.2
1988	13.0	5.6
1989	8.8	14.9
1990	−7.1	−2.5
1991	23.2	6.0
1992	6.7	−2.0
1993	6.6	6.1

Source: Merrill Lynch Quantitative Analysis

Betas are often adjusted to be more predictive or forward-looking because their values tend to gravitate toward 1.0. Higher beta stocks tend to become lower beta stocks, and lower beta stocks tend to become higher beta stocks. Figure 6.12 examines the betas of the Consumer Staples and Energy sectors from 1980 to 1993. The businesses of these two sectors are quite different, with their successes being somewhat inversely correlated. If energy prices rise, then inflation tends to rise as well, and that has historically meant that profit margins in the Consumer Staples sector get squeezed. Entering the 1980s, the Energy sector was generally considered to be a superior performing sector, while the Consumer Staples sector was considered to be a "dog" because of the 1970s inflation. The 1980s, however, were generally a period of falling energy prices and disinflation, and the Consumer Staples sector became one of the growth areas of the decade, while the Energy sector was basically in a depression. The result was that the beta of the Consumer Staples sector generally rose through the decade (from 0.80 to 1.06), while that of the Energy sector fell (from a high of 1.20 to a low of 0.68 in 1992). The trends of the betas of these two sectors has a correlation of −0.93.

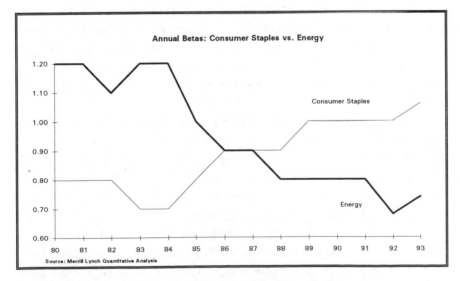

Figure 6.12   Annual Betas: Consumer Staples vs. Energy

With future growth prospects questionable, the dividend yield of the Energy sector, which was actually lower than that of the overall S&P 500 in 1980 (3.6 percent versus 4.8 percent for the S&P 500 in December 1980), finished 1993 with a yield about 50 percent higher than that of the overall market. The Consumer Staples sector had a dividend yield that was higher than both the Energy sector and the S&P 500 in 1980 (5.8 percent), but had a dividend yield less that of the S&P 500 by year-end 1993. Those changes in yield arose largely because of the perception that growth could, in the case of the Consumer Staples, or could not, in the case of the Energy sector, be generated internally in an environment without inflation.

A widely accepted method for adjusting betas to be more predictive is the Blume method, cited earlier, which is based on beta's tendency to gravitate toward 1.00. Blume examined betas during disparate time periods and found that an appropriate formula to estimate that regression to 1.0 was as follows:

$$\text{Beta}_{\text{Predicted}} = 0.677(\text{Beta}_{\text{Historical}}) + 0.343$$

Vasicek (1973) has suggested a similar method for forecasting betas, but rather than adjust all betas by the same amount, he notes that betas should be adjusted by the probabilistic uncertainty surrounding the historical beta. Statisticians refer to that type of adjustment as a Bayesian adjustment. Elton and Gruber (1984) point out several studies that demonstrate that both the Blume and Bayesian adjustments are better predictors of future betas than are the simple historical betas.

An important question for the manager interested in market segments defined by beta is what factors cause changes in the slope of the Security Market Line. Why was the Security Market Line downward sloping or flat during the 1980s, and what might affect that slope in the future? If the line were to remain downward sloping, then there might be little reason to form high beta portfolios except as potential short portfolios. However, if the slope of the line is going to revert to one that reflects more traditional risk/ return relationships, then one would want to hold high beta portfolios. The interrelationships between beta and such other factors as quality, size, and yield have been discussed. The factors that alter the performance of market segments according to those other factors explain much of what occurred during the 1980s with respect to beta and the slope of the Security Market Line.

Chapter 2 highlighted that the product bought and sold within the equity market is nominal profits growth, and that the abundance or scarcity of such growth results in cycles of performance between growth and value and high quality and low quality. A similar relationship exists for high and low beta companies in which higher beta companies will tend to outperform as expectations for nominal profits growth become more optimistic. The slope of the security market line may be highly dependent on expectations of nominal profits growth. If nominal profits growth is expected to improve, then the Security Market Line may begin to slope more steeply. However, if nominal profits growth is expected to become more scarce, then the line may flatten or slope downward.

The returns of lower beta companies tend to be more stable, like utilities or Consumer Staples in 1980, because their growth opportunities are fewer than those of other companies. They, therefore, tend to pay out a larger proportion of their earnings to shareholders as cash dividends, with cash being a zero beta asset. If nominal growth rates are expected to improve, then almost by definition, the marginal increase in growth must come from the less stable, economically sensitive companies. As expectations for nominal growth change, it is the marginal growth opportunity that either appears or disappears. Simply put, stable companies are indeed stable, while higher beta, less stable companies are the firms that respond, whether positively or negatively, to changes in nominal profits growth and to changes in investors' expectations regarding that growth.

If that is true, then how can one explain the 1980s during which the stocks of stable companies became growth stocks? That answer lies in Figure 6.12, which showed the betas of the Consumer Staples and Energy sectors through time. When inflation was finally squeezed out of the U.S. economy, a large group of companies, which never truly had the opportunity to look for growth opportunities because their margins were squeezed by inflation, suddenly

found expanding margins, while many companies that used inflation as a source of nominal earnings growth suddenly found that
growth opportunities were difficult to justify. The yield (which
inversely reflects growth opportunities) of the Consumer Staples
sector was higher, and the yield of the Energy sector lower than
that of the S&P 500 during 1980, but that yield differential had
reversed by 1993. Consumer Staples companies found an increasing number of projects that appeared to offer high return on investment, while companies within the Energy sector could not. In
fact, companies within the Energy sector had the larger problem
that many of their existing projects were providing negative return
on investment.

Thus, disinflation may be the main reason that the Security
Market Line became flat to downward sloping during the 1980s.
Of course, had the U.S. economy been able to keep nominal growth
rates high through productivity, then the line might have remained
upward sloping. Actually, productivity rates declined during parts
of the 1980s.

That reasoning suggests that higher beta companies did not
outperform during the 1980s because the building inflation of the
1970s led investor expectations for high beta stocks to be too optimistic, and expectations for low beta stocks to be overly pessimistic as investors entered the 1980s. In other words, high beta
stocks might have been at midnight on the Earnings Expectations
Life Cycle during the early 1980s, while low beta stocks were at
six o'clock. It should be clear why lower beta companies outperformed higher beta companies during the 1980s: Investors slowly,
but surely, realized that growth opportunities and returns were
superior among more stable companies.

As Figure 6.12, which compared the betas of the Consumer
Staples and Energy sectors, pointed out, however, some of what
were once quite stable companies no longer appear to be so stable.
The situation that faced investors during the early 1980s may be
in the process of being reversed, and the market may be returning
to more traditional risk/return relationships. It may be that the
expectations regarding so-called stable companies may be overly
optimistic in light of the fact that they may not be so stable any-

more. Such stocks may now be at midnight on the Life Cycle. Real and nominal growth rates in the U.S. economy are strengthening, and that may mean that the growth opportunities may shift again toward "traditional" high beta stocks.

Table 6.4 shows the betas for various market economic sectors and market segments. Note that Conglomerates, which are diversified companies that attempt to hold a portfolio of businesses, is the sector that has the beta closest to 1.00. That occurs because the portfolio of businesses concept forces broader than normal diversification of corporate assets that ultimately makes the group mirror the overall market. High beta, economically sensitive sectors, such as Credit Cyclicals, Transportation, Capital Goods, and Technology might perform well if the Security Market Line were to again slope upward.

◆ *Summary*

- ◆ Beta is a traditional measure of risk that calculates the risk of a stock within the context of a well-diversified portfolio.

Table 6.4   Market Segment Betas

Segment/Sector	Beta as of 12/31/93
Credit Cyclical	1.33
Financial	1.22
Transportation	1.17
Capital Goods	1.15
Consumer Growth Staples	1.13
Technology	1.13
Basic Industries	1.06
Consumer Cyclicals	1.06
Consumer Staples	1.06
Conglomerates	1.01
Utilities	0.80
Energy	0.74

Source: Merrill Lynch Quantitative Analysis

- ◆ A stock's total risk can be divided into firm-specific risk and nondiversifiable (beta) risk. Firm-specific risks tend to cancel out within a portfolio.

- ◆ Higher yielding, larger, and more asset-stable companies tend to have lower betas, while lower yielding, smaller, higher projected growth and lower-quality companies tend to have higher betas.

- ◆ Traditional theory suggests that beta should be a good predictor of returns because investors should be compensated for taking additional risk. That atypically did not happen during the 1980s, but it appears as though traditional risk/return relationships are returning.

- ◆ The performance of higher beta companies tends to improve as expectations for nominal earnings growth improve. When earnings growth improves, that improvement tends to come from riskier companies, while the earnings growth of safer companies tends to remain more stable.

- ◆ The washing out of inflation from the U.S. economy during the 1980s, and the resulting declines in nominal growth rates, may explain why higher beta stocks underperformed during that period.

- ◆ Betas are not stable and tend to gravitate toward 1.0. Higher beta stocks in one period will not necessarily be high beta stocks during the next. Similarly, lower betas may increase through time.

- ◆ Investors should be aware of how performance, expectations, and overreaction can influence the calculation of a company's beta.

◆ References

Baskin, Jonathan, "Dividend Policy and the Volatility of Common Stocks," *Journal of Portfolio Management*, Spring 1989, pp. 19–25.

Bernstein, Richard and Pradhuman, Satya, "Risk & Return Return," *Merrill Lynch Quantitative Viewpoint*, July 27, 1993.

Bernstein, Richard and Pradhuman, Satya, "Are Defensive Stocks 'Defensive?' " *Merrill Lynch Quantitative Analysis Update*, March 10, 1994.

Blume, Marshall, "Betas and Their Regression Tendencies," *Journal of Finance*, June 1975, vol. X, no. 3, pp. 785–795.

Chan, Louis K. C. and Lakonishok, Josef, "Are the Reports of Beta's Death Premature?" *Journal of Portfolio Management*, Summer 1993, pp. 51–62.

Elton, Edwin J. and Gruber, Martin J., *Portfolio Theory and Investment Analysis* (New York: John Wiley & Sons), 1984.

Fama, Eugene F. and French, Kenneth R., "Cross-Sectional Variation in Expected Stock Returns," *Journal of Finance*, vol. XLVII, 1992.

Gordon, M.J., "Optimal Investment and Financing Policy," *Journal of Finance*, May 1963, pp. 264–272.

Grinold, Richard, "Is Beta Dead Again?" *Financial Analysts Journal*, July/August 1993, pp. 28–34.

Miller, M. and Modigliani, F., "Dividend Policy, Growth, and the Valuation of Shares," *Journal of Business*, October 1961, pp. 411–433.

Sharpe, William F., *Portfolio Theory and Capital Markets* (New York: McGraw-Hill), 1970.

Vasicek, Oldrich, "A Note on Using Cross-Sectional Information in Bayesian Estimation of Security Betas," *Journal of Finance*, December 1973, vol. VIII, no. 5, pp. 1233–1239.

7

Dividend Yield and Equity Duration

◆

 ost investors realize that the
stock market is sensitive to changes in interest rates. Stock prices
tend to decrease when interest rates rise, and they tend to rise
when interest rates fall. While some academics have suggested that
excess volatility in the equity markets may be attributable to irrational fads and speculative bubbles (Shiller, 1989), some practitioners (perhaps for reasons discussed in Chapter 3) have alter-
natively suggested that such excess volatility might be attributable
to changes in interest rates (Spiro, 1990). While this book is largely
based on investor behavior, one cannot ignore the impact that interest rates do have on equity market volatility.

Style investors need to concern themselves with the interest
rate sensitivity of individual segments, sectors, and stocks because
segments react differently to changes in interest rates. While the
performance of some sectors of the equity market is almost totally
controlled by interest rate movements, other sectors' interest sensitivity is muted by other, more powerful factors. Thus, when the
stock market rises or falls because of interest rates, different investment styles can potentially have vastly different performances.
This chapter examines the measurement of interest rate sensitivity,
how interest rates affect different styles of investing, and the mit-
igating factors that can offset the interest rate sensitivities that are
imbedded into certain investment styles. In addition, this chapter

will also lay the groundwork for several of the topics discussed in Chapter 8 on large versus small stock investing.

Dividend yield is a common definition of market segments, and some portfolio managers require stocks to have a certain dividend yield before considering them for investment. It is often thought that dividend yield and interest rate sensitivity must go hand in hand because higher dividend yielding stocks act more "bond-like." One of the goals of this chapter is to dispel that common thought. Higher yielding stocks are not necessarily more interest sensitive than are lower yielding stocks.

Interest rate sensitivity is commonly called *duration.* The term duration is usually associated with fixed-income investments, and refers to the change in an instrument's return for a one percentage point interest rate move. Essentially, the measurement of interest rate sensitivity demonstrates not only how much return an investor might expect to get from an investment, but also *when* one might expect to receive it.

Because of the attempt to measure when returns are received, duration can be thought of as the weighted average maturity of a bond, and is typically measured in years. Longer duration assets will tend to be more interest rate sensitive, and shorter duration instruments less so. The yield-to-maturity of a bond is the internal rate of return that equates today's bond price with the coupon and principle payments to be received in the future. Two thirty-year government bonds may have nearly the same yield-to-maturity, but if one is a zero coupon bond, while the other is a coupon bearing bond, duration analysis suggests that these two bonds, although having the same yield-to-maturity and maturity date, will not perform identically when interest rates change. The coupon bearing bond rewards the investor over the thirty-year period, while the zero coupon bond rewards the investor only in the thirtieth year. The coupon bearing bond has a shorter weighted average maturity of cash flows than does the zero coupon bond. We will shortly examine the details of why that is so.

There are many factors that influence a bond's duration. Maturity, coupon, yield, and credit rating all can influence the duration calculation. Table 7.1 summarizes some of the major influences.

Table 7.1 Some Factors That Influence Duration

Factor	Change in Factor	Change in Duration
Coupon	Higher	Shorter
Yield	Higher	Shorter
Maturity	Longer	Longer
Credit Rating	Lower	Shorter

As mentioned in the previous example, higher coupon bonds will tend to have shorter durations than will lower coupon bonds, all other things being equal. Higher coupon payments suggest that the investor receives more return sooner than would an investor in low or zero coupon bonds. Higher near-term cash flows will tend to shorten duration.

Higher current yields also suggest shorter durations for reasons similar to that described for the higher coupon bonds. However, current yield better reflects investors' attitudes toward the particular bond. For example, a bond with a 7 percent coupon might have a current yield of 6 percent or 8 percent if investors had bid the bond's price up or down. All other things being equal, bonds with higher coupons will have shorter durations because the investor will be receiving more cash flow sooner.

Longer maturity bonds will tend to have longer durations than will bonds of similar coupon, yield, and credit rating, but with shorter maturities. That occurs because the cash flows, although equal to those of the shorter maturity bond, are spread out over a longer time period. Cash flows might be similar, but they will be received later rather than sooner and, thus, duration is longer.

Finally, a bond with a lower credit rating is generally a shorter duration bond, all other things being equal. That occurs because investors usually must be compensated for the lower quality bond's default risk with a higher coupon or current yield. That higher coupon is a function of risk and return similar to that discussed in Chapter 6. If the characteristics of two bonds were identical in every way, but one was rated AAA while the other was rated B, rational investors would naturally choose the AAA bond because they were not being paid to accept the potential default risk associated with the B bond. Compensation for that additional risk is the higher coupon associated with the lower-quality bond, which results in a larger payment sooner, and effectively shortens duration.

Additionally, higher coupon bonds are generally less affected by rising interest rates than are lower coupon bonds because higher coupon bonds are often found among more economically sensitive sectors, and the stimulus for rising interest rates is a strengthening nominal economy. Thus, the default and economic risks associated with lower coupon bonds tend to dissipate as interest rates rise. Investors begin to arbitrage away the risk/return advantage offered by higher coupon bonds at that point in the economic cycle, and the bonds outperform in a rising interest rate environment.

There are many other factors besides its duration that can influence a bond's total return such as call dates, sinking fund provisions, floating rates, prepayments, and convexity (how duration changes as interest rates change). However, these topics are beyond the scope of this book, and the interested reader is directed toward the bond mathematics texts and articles that are referenced at the end of the chapter.

The formal calculation for duration originates from the yield-to-maturity formula, and time weights the present value of the individual coupons. The standard bond yield-to-maturity formula is as follows:

Bond Price =
$$C_1/(1+YTM) + C_2/(1+YTM)^2 + \ldots$$
$$+ (C_n+P)/(1+YTM)^n,$$

where,
C = coupon in a given year,
P = principal payment,
n = length of time until maturity,
YTM = Yield-to-maturity.

The standard duration formula (developed by Macaulay, 1938) time weights the present values of the individual coupon payments within the yield-to-maturity formula:

$$D = ((C_1*1)/(1+YTM))/(C_1/(1+YTM)) +$$
$$((C_2*2)/(1+YTM)^2)/(C_2/(1+YTM)^2) +$$
$$\ldots +$$
$$(((C_n+P)*n)/(1+YTM)^n)/(C_n/(1+YTM)^n),$$

where,

C = Coupon,

P = Principal,

YTM = Yield-to-Maturity,

n = length of time to maturity.

Using that formula for duration, it becomes apparent that, because there are no interim cash payments, the duration of a zero coupon instrument is simply its maturity, and that higher interim payments serve to shorten duration.

Duration has become more closely associated with equities over the past decade. As interest rates became more volatile during the 1980s, an increasingly larger number of equity investors began to realize how significantly interest rates could affect equity returns. Those large declines in interest rates forced plan sponsors to reevaluate their asset/liability matching schemes. Asset/liability actuaries began to use lower discount rates as the overall level of interest rates fell, and using a lower discount rate meant that the present value of any future liabilities began to increase. Thus, forced with rising anticipated liabilities and new FASB accounting regulations regarding pension underfunding, corporations began to shift their pension asset allocations toward higher returning assets such as equities. Duration analysis was one method to determine how equities contributed to or detracted from asset/liability matches. There are three generally accepted methods for calculating equity duration, and we will begin with the simplest one first.

Some investors define equity duration simply as the inverse of the dividend yield. Stocks offering higher dividend yields will, therefore, have shorter durations, while stocks offering little or no yield will have longer durations. The theory behind this definition is straightforward: The investor assumes that interim cash flow payments (namely, a stock's dividends) will remain at today's level forever so that the dividends resemble a perpetuity. This may sound simplistic, but it is a good intuitive approach upon which to base the subsequent more sophisticated equity duration measures.

The duration of a perpetuity is the inverse of its yield-to-maturity, and thus the formula for the duration of a perpetuity is:

$$D = (1+YTM)/YTM$$
$$\text{where, } D = \text{duration, and}$$
$$YTM = \text{yield-to-maturity.}$$

Similarly, the duration of an equity perpetuity would be the inverse of its dividend yield or price divided by dividend. Whereas the dividend yield of a stock is calculated by dividing the dividend by price (D/P*100), duration would be measured as price divided by dividend (P/D*100).

Essentially, the inverse of the dividend yield method assumes that companies with high P/E ratios and low dividend yields have long durations, while those stocks with low P/E ratios and high dividend yields have short durations. If one assumes a constant world in which P/E ratios, earnings, and dividend yields do not change, then the number of years of earnings that the company must produce for the investor to recoup his or her initial price is the P/E itself. For example, if an investor pays $25 for a stock and the company's earnings are $5 per share, then it will take the investor five years of earnings to equal the initial $25. It would, therefore, take an investor a long time to recoup the earnings for a very high P/E stock, but only a few years for those of the low P/E stock. Meanwhile, the company may be paying out some proportion of those earnings in the form of dividends. A company with a low P/E and high dividend yield can be thought of as a shorter-term instrument with a higher coupon, while the high P/E stock that pays no dividends can be thought of more as a zero coupon bond.

The problem with the inverse of the dividend yield duration measure is that it assumes that the cash flows in the future will remain identical to today's. The Dividend Discount Model (DDM), a widely used equity valuation model that allows estimated future earnings and cash flows to change through time, originated from the same discounted cash flow analysis that was the base for the bond yield-to-maturity formula. The DDM replaces the yield-to-maturity formula's coupons with an estimated future dividend stream, and equates the stock's present value (price) to that future dividend stream. Instead of calling the internal rate of return that equates the price to the future stream of cash flows a yield-to-maturity as do bond investors, equity investors refer to it as an expected return.

The formula for the DDM is very similar to the yield-to-maturity formula, and is as follows:

Stock Price =
$$D_1/(1+r) + D_2/(1+r)^2 + D_3/(1+r)^3 + \ldots ,$$
where,
D = estimated dividend payment in a given year,
r = expected return.

Given the similarity between the yield-to-maturity formula and the DDM, the DDM can obviously be altered to calculate equity duration similar to the way the yield-to-maturity formula can be altered to calculate bond duration.

The advantage to this duration calculation over the inverse of the dividend yield calculation is that the DDM does not necessarily assume that future cash flows are constant, and thus permits a more dynamic valuation calculation. The difference between the two calculations is minor for mature companies with dimmer growth prospects because the future cash flows do indeed tend to resemble a perpetuity. For example, the estimated future dividend streams for most utilities are generally quite flat. However, the difference can be quite large for smaller companies with significant future growth prospects or for cyclical companies whose growth prospects might be better during an expanding economy. The DDM methodology tends to lengthen the duration of mature companies, while it shortens the durations of younger companies.

Figure 7.1 highlights the typical assumed earnings growth rates within a DDM. The projected earnings growth rates for a

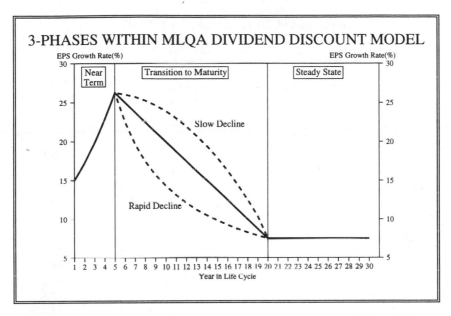

Figure 7.1 Earnings Growth Rates within a DDM

utility would be much flatter, which would imply similar flatness for the company's dividends as well. The projected pattern for a growth stock might be considerably steeper in the near term period, and might decline more slowly during a longer transition phase.

Table 7.2, shown earlier in Chapter 4, further demonstrates the differences between these two measures of duration. Note that the measures for Utilities barely change, while the measures for "Small" Stocks and "Growth" Stocks change significantly.

The relationship between duration and P/E is similar, however, regardless of the duration calculation used. Figures 7.2 and 7.3 show the relationship between the durations of the segments and sectors highlighted in the previous table with their P/E ratios. In both cases, the regression line between duration and P/E is indeed upward sloping, indicating that higher P/Es and longer durations tend to go together.

The third measure of duration, proposed by Leibowitz, et al. (1978, 1986, 1989, 1993) attempts to calculate a more "pure" measure of interest rate sensitivity. Whereas duration measures derived from the DDM are generally in the twenty- and thirty-year range,

Table 7.2   Sector/Segment Duration as of 12/31/93

Sector/Segment	DDM Duration	Inv. of Yield
Transportation	38.9	71.4
DDM "Overvalued" Stocks	38.9	52.6
Credit Cyclicals	35.9	66.7
Technology	35.6	90.9
Consumer Cyclicals	32.8	55.6
Basic Industrials	32.6	40.0
"Small" Stocks	32.1	90.9
"Mid-Cap" Stocks	30.8	45.4
Conglomerates	30.1	38.5
Financial	29.8	38.5
Consumer Growth Staples	29.7	71.4
"Growth" Stocks	29.3	66.7
S&P 500	**28.5**	**40.0**
"Large" Stocks	28.2	38.5
Capital Goods	28.2	47.6
Consumer Staples	25.0	47.6
Energy	24.9	27.8
DDM "Undervalued" Stocks	23.2	33.3
"Defensive" Stocks	22.3	21.7
Utilities	22.0	21.7

Source: Merrill Lynch Quantitative Analysis

historical durations, meaning the actual historical changes in stock returns as a result of past interest rate changes, are more on the order of five to ten years. This method attempts to account for that difference between observed and DDM durations by controlling for other factors such as inflation.

Leibowitz, et al. (1989) argue that the traditional DDM-type measures of equity duration do not allow for any interaction between the discount rate and the other variables within the DDM. For example, dividend estimates might rise as inflation rises, but as inflation rises so might the discount rate. They suggest that the DDM version of duration focuses solely on the single discount rate variable. The DDM-based measure of duration is based on the traditional fixed-income methods, but the interaction between variables within the formula is moot for most fixed-income instruments because, as their name implies, their cash flows are fixed. With the

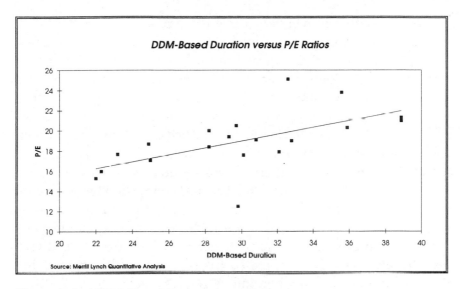

Figure 7.2 DDM-Based Duration vs. P/E

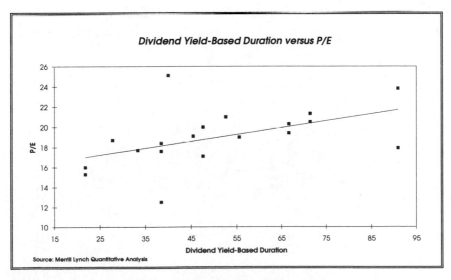

Figure 7.3 Dividend Yield-Based Duration vs. P/E

exception of those elements that might affect various types of floating rate notes, there are no interactions between the cash flows and the discount rate for most fixed-income securities. If interest rates rise or fall enough because of strength or weakness in the economy, then investors do raise questions regarding the success or bankruptcy potential of the company. While those situations can be viewed as a dramatic change in *expected* cash flows, cash flows for a bond are fixed according to the covenants of the bond. Dividend payments, however, are obviously quite variable.

Figure 7.4 demonstrates the historical connection between dividend growth and inflation rates by examining the changes in those rates through time. (Note that we have used simple moving averages to smooth the series for graphing purposes). Dividend growth rates have indeed tended to rise when inflation rates increased, and decreased when inflation subsided.

Table 7.3 shows the historical relationships, or observed durations, between various industry groups and interest rates. It also shows the effect a one percentage point *increase* in interest rates has historically had on the industry groups' capital appreciation

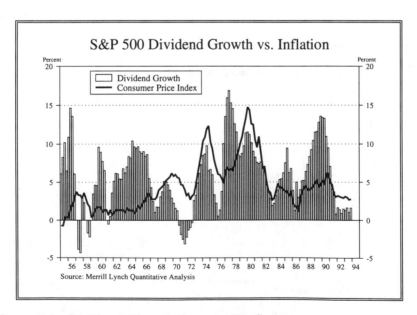

Figure 7.4 Dividend Growth Rates and Inflation

Table 7.3   Observed Interest Rates Sensitivities

S&P Industry Group Index	*Observed Durations*
Savings & Loans	−13.0
Retail-Gen. Merchandising	−7.5
Household Products	−5.7
Money Center Banks	−5.6
Electric Utilities	−5.5
Life Insurance	−5.3
Autos	−5.1
Foods	−5.0
Beverages—Alcoholic	−5.0
S&P 500	−4.7
Beverages—Soft Drinks	−4.5
Retail—Dept. Stores	−4.4
S&P Financial Index—Cosmetics	−3.9
Building Materials	−3.6
Truckers	−3.5
Biotechnology(*)	−3.4
Property/Casualty Insurance	−2.9
S&P Consumer Goods Index	−2.8
Regional Banks	−2.7
Chemicals	−1.4
Drugs	−1.2
Tobacco	−1.1
S&P Capital Goods Index	−0.1
Conglomerates	+2.0
Railroads	+3.3
Oil—International	+3.9
Aluminum	+4.1
Steel	+4.4
Machinery	+5.3
Oil—Domestic	+5.7
Misc. Metals	+9.3
Machine Tools	+9.9
Oil Well Eq. & Service	+11.5
Gold	+13.1

NOTE: Observed durations are the 12-month percentage change in the historical industry group performance for a one percentage point change over a 12-month period in long-term interest rates (10+ Years T-Bond) from 1974 to 1993.

(*) Biotechnology index constructed by Merrill Lynch Quantitative Analysis, which was available only from 1986 to 1993.

Source: Merrill Lynch Quantitative Analysis

when one removes the influence that interest rates have had on the overall equity market. The table lists those industries that have been most negatively affected by interest rate increases to those that have been affected the least. Note that the least interest rate sensitive groups are actually positively correlated with interest rates. That means that their relative returns versus the overall market have historically increased on average when interest rates have increased.

The table demonstrates that more stable, less economically sensitive industries (such as Household Products, Soft Drinks, and Foods) tend to be more interest rate sensitive than are more economically sensitive industries (such as Steels, Machine Tools, or Metals). Oil price inflation and deflation was a major determinant of interest rates over the period studied. Thus, oil-related industries appear at the bottom of the table. Gold stocks, a traditional hedge against inflation, is the industry with the most positive relationship to interest rate increases because gold prices tend to anticipate inflation as do long-term interest rates.

Interest rate sensitivity and dividend yield do not go hand in hand as is commonly thought. Figure 7.5 demonstrates that the

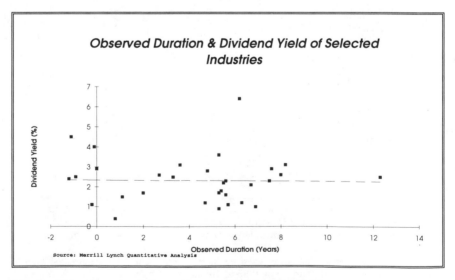

Figure 7.5 Observed Duration and Dividend Yield

dividend yields associated with the industries just discussed do not correlate well with the industries' observed durations. The line in the figure indicates the regression between observed duration and dividend yield, and its flatness implies that dividend yield has almost no relationship with observed duration. The results of this analysis seem to refute the common notion that higher yielding stocks must be more interest rate sensitive.

Inflation, as mentioned in several previous chapters, can be an important stimulant to a company's nominal earnings growth, but inflation does not uniformly affect companies. Some companies benefit greatly from inflation because their profits are more dependent on the firm's ability to raise prices. If inflation is muted, then only the company with a product in great demand can raise prices; a company that produces a marginal product or a commodity that can easily be produced without any proprietary production process probably cannot. However, if the general inflation rate is rising, then the marginal product's or commodity's price can more easily be raised. While inflation generally helps producers of marginal products or commodities, inflation can also squeeze some company's profit margins because they cannot pass on price increases to their customers despite the rising prices of their raw materials.

There have been many studies regarding industries' abilities to pass along or "flow through" inflation, and whether the stocks of those industries might make good hedges against inflation. Asikoglu and Ercan (1992) and Ma and Ellis (1989) are two of the more recent studies. Both studies highlighted that empirical data suggested significant differences among companies, and that some companies or industries have historically been able to pass along the effects of inflation, while others clearly have not. Companies may be less affected by inflation because of their capital structures and efficiency. For others, it may simply be that the bottlenecks within the economy from which inflation has historically originated are in those industries. While financial assets in general tend not to perform well during periods of inflation, they found that the stock prices of companies that can pass along or adapt to inflation tend to be less adversely affected.

The Leibowitz measure of equity duration attempts to purify the interest rate sensitivity of a stock, and to account for that inflation pass-through effect. The highlighted studies point out that inflation tends to drive up interest rates, but that some companies might actually benefit from that inflation, and thus their earnings growth might offset the increase in interest rates pointing to a shortfall in the DDM version of duration. The formula for the Leibowitz measure of duration follows, and is presented as the sensitivity of a stock to real interest rates, DDM-based duration, and inflation pass-through.

$$\text{Price Change} = -D_{DDM}(1-\gamma + dh/dr)dr-$$
$$D_{DDM}(1-\lambda + dh/dI)dI,$$

where,

D_{DDM} = DDM-based duration measure,

γ = the growth rate sensitivity to real interest rates,

h = equity market risk premium,

r = real component of nominal rates,

λ = an inflation pass-through parameter,

I = inflation component of nominal rates.

Whereas the DDM version of duration assumes that estimated future cash flows remain the same relative to changes in inflation, the Leibowitz duration allows for changing cash flows because of changes in inflation. Thus, industries that have a high inflation pass-through tend to experience a shortening of duration when interest rates rise because of increases in inflation. A hypothetical example of the influence of the inflation pass-through variable in the duration formula might be seen in a comparison of biotechnology stocks and aluminum stocks. At the trough of a recession, both the biotechnology and the aluminum stock will have a very long duration. The biotechnology stock might have a long duration because the company has no viable products and, thus, no near-term cash flows. The stock's multiple to earnings and cash flow would probably be infinite. The aluminum company may have a long duration because the recession has caused near-term business prospects to be quite dim, and the company might well be operating at a significant loss. Its valuation multiples, like those of the biotechnology company, might be infinite. The difference between these two stocks is that, if the economy did improve, then the aluminum company's cash flows would quickly improve because aluminum companies are highly economically sensitive. The cash flows of the biotechnology company probably would not change at all because the biotechnology company is not economically sensitive. Thus, if interest rates began to rise as the economic cycle matured, the aluminum company would be less adversely affected because its overall duration would be shortening at the same time.

In addition, the Leibowitz formula for duration also adjusts for companies that are adversely affected by increases in interest rates (real rates to be more precise). Companies in the financial sector, or that might have higher debt levels, might also have accentuated interest rate sensitivity beyond what the DDM-based version might imply. Table 7.4 attempts to summarize the effects of the Leibowitz duration measure.

Bernstein (1992) suggests that the additional information provided by the Leibowitz duration measure may be a more sophisticated way of measuring the probability of earnings surprises at certain points in the economic cycle. Durations for economically

Table 7.4 Summary of Leibowitz Equity Duration

Variable	Discussion
D_{DDM}	Longer DDM-based durations imply longer Leibowitz duration.
γ	Higher γ implies that estimated growth rates are more sensitive to real interest rates, which implies longer Leibowitz duration.
dh/dr	A higher equity risk premium relative to interest rates implies a longer Leibowitz duration.
λ	The more able a company is to pass-through inflation, the shorter the Leibowitz duration.
dh/dI	A higher equity risk premium relative to inflation implies a longer Leibowitz duration.

sensitive stocks are often extremely long at the trough of a recession because current earnings are depressed and analyst earnings expectations for future growth prospects are usually at their most bearish extreme. As the economy recovers and nominal growth rates begin to improve, the probability of positive earnings surprises is the largest among stocks for which no one is enthusiastic. The exact opposite would be true at the peak of an economic cycle. The portion of the Leibowitz duration measure that focuses on inflation pass-through sensitivity may, therefore, be a good proxy for gauging potential positive surprise candidates at some points of the economic cycle.

Duration and dividend yield play an important role in style investment because interest rates set the benchmark for discounting future nominal growth. As interest rates fall, longer duration assets will tend to outperform. In the equity world, that generally means that higher P/E, lower yielding stocks will outperform. But, when interest rates rise, shorter duration assets will outperform. That generally implies that lower P/E, higher yielding stocks with greater earnings potential will outperform.

The relationship between interest rates, duration, and equity performance has a significant impact on the performance of growth and value strategies. Table 7.5, taken from Bernstein (1992), shows the DDM-based durations for several growth- and value-oriented strategies. Value strategies, in general, tend to be lower duration strategies, and therefore, less interest rate sensitive than are growth strategies.

Portfolios formed using such strategies tend to have durations that mirror the numbers in Table 7.5. Observed durations among a set of growth and value managers support that contention. Table 7.6 shows the observed durations of the growth and value managers highlighted in Chapter 4. Growth mutual funds tended to be more interest rate sensitive than were value mutual funds during the periods studied.

Chapter 8 will focus on market segments determined by company size. Smaller capitalization stocks generally performed quite poorly during the 1980s and, as was mentioned in Chapter 6, that has led some to question the value of the Capital Asset Pricing

Table 7.5 DDM-Based Durations for Growth and Value Strategies as of 8/31/92

Strategy	DDM-Based Duration
Value	
High EPS Yield	21.0 Years
High DDM Alpha	23.0
Low Price/Sales	26.7
Low Price/Cash Flow	26.8
Low Price/Book Value	27.1
Growth	
Positive EPS Surprise	27.7
High EPS Momentum	28.2
High Projected 5-Year Growth	31.1
Upward EPS Estimate Revision	32.7
Equal-Weighted S&P 500	27.8

Source: Merrill Lynch Quantitative Analysis

Table 7.6 Observed Durations of Growth and Value Mutual Funds

Type of Fund	Jan '82–July '92	Jan '87–July '92
Growth Funds	525 bp	558bp
Value Funds	371 bp	318bp
Difference	154bp	240bp

NOTE: Figures in the table represent the impact on the funds' change in net asset value as a result of a one percentage point move in long-term interest rates (10+ Years).
Source: Merrill Lynch Quantitative Analysis

Model because smaller stocks tend to have higher betas. However, duration analysis might also be helpful in explaining their under-performance during that time period. Bernstein and Tew (1991) suggest that the underperformance of smaller capitalization stocks during the 1980s might be attributable to their low growth rates relative to their duration risk. They suggest that shorter duration stocks offered investors competitive (and often superior) nominal earnings growth to that offered by longer duration stocks. Given the choice of taking duration risk or not taking duration risk, but yet potentially receiving the same amount of nominal growth, investors gravitated toward shorter duration equities.

They further suggest that duration is a measure of the "certainty of return." There are two parts to a stock's total return, namely its dividend yield and it capital appreciation. Investors are relatively certain regarding the total return attributable to dividend yield because they know the date they will receive it and, within some guidelines, what the amount will be. Capital appreciation, on the other hand, is relatively uncertain. Although investors approach stocks with expectations, they do not know the amount of capital appreciation they will receive or when they will receive it. Bernstein and Tew suggest that certain stocks are the T-Bills and the T-Bonds of the equity world. Thus, similar to T-Bills yielding the same as T-Bonds, if short duration stocks offer competitive growth rates to longer duration stocks, investors will rationally shift toward the shorter duration stocks because their returns are not only similar to those of longer duration stocks, but also relatively more certain.

Bernstein and Tew go on to suggest that there is a "yield curve" within the equity market that represents the tradeoff between expected growth and duration risk. They hypothesize that similar to the fixed-income yield curve, the equity yield curve should generally be upward sloping in order to entice investors to take duration risk. They demonstrate that the equity yield curve was relatively flat during much of the 1980s, and speculate whether that abnormal tradeoff contributed to the underperformance of smaller capitalization stocks. At the time, they suggested that the curve would have to be more upward sloping for small stocks to outperform.

Figure 7.6 compares several equity yield curves from June 1989 and May 1990. One can see that the curve does indeed change slope, and that it subsequently did become more upward sloping prior to the small stock rally that began in late 1990. We will see in the next chapter that duration and nominal growth expectations are a major determinant of the performance of smaller capitalization stocks.

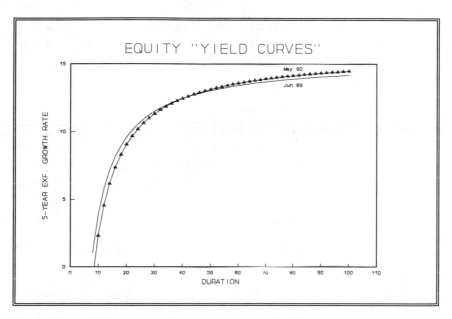

Figure 7.6 Selected Equity "Yield Curves"

◆ *Summary*

- ◆ Duration is a measure of interest rate sensitivity that has traditionally been reserved for fixed-income instruments, but more recently has been applied to equities.

- ◆ Duration measures the change in return relative to a one percentage point change in interest rates.

- ◆ There are three methods to measure equity duration: the inverse of the dividend yield, the DDM-based version, and what we have called the Leibowitz method.

- ◆ The inverse of the dividend yield is intuitively pleasing, but assumes constant expectations.

- ◆ The DDM-based version is the most similar to the fixed-income calculation, and is more defensible than is the inverse of the dividend yield because it is based on a stream of expectations that are not assumed to be constant.

♦ The problem with the DDM-based duration measure is that it suggests equity durations generally in the range of twenty to thirty years. Observed durations tend to be between five and ten years.

♦ The Leibowitz measure of duration attempts to reconcile the DDM-based and observed durations by measuring various sensitivities to nominal growth and to real interest rates. As the economy grows more strongly, interest rates will tend to rise. However, some companies will benefit from that economic growth more than others and their durations will tend to shorten.

♦ Contrary to popular thought, higher yielding stocks are not necessarily more interest rate sensitive.

♦ Growth strategies tend to have longer durations than do value strategies.

♦ Duration analysis may be helpful in explaining the underperformance of smaller capitalization stocks during the 1980s because, during that period, shorter duration stocks offered similar potential growth to that offered by longer duration stocks.

♦ Duration can also be thought of as a measure of the "certainty of return." Given similar expected returns, the rational investor should probably invest in the shorter duration asset because the return is more certain.

♦ It has been suggested that there is a yield curve within the equity market that relates duration to expected nominal growth. The shape and slope of that yield curve may lend insight regarding the willingness of investors to take risk.

♦ References

Asikoglu, Yaman and Ercan, Metin R., "Inflation Flow-Through and Stock Prices," *Journal of Portfolio Management*, Spring 1992, pp. 63–68.

Baskin, Jonathan, "Dividend Policy and the Volatility of Common Stocks," *Journal of Portfolio Management*, Spring 1989, pp. 19–25.

Bernstein, Richard, "The Growth/Duration Matrix: Opportunities for Tilting and Arbitrage," *Merrill Lynch Quantitative Viewpoint*, February 27, 1990.

Bernstein, Richard, "A Bond Investor's Guide to Equities and Duration," *Merrill Lynch Quantitative Viewpoint*, February 25, 1992.

Bernstein, Richard, "Managing Equities Like Bonds, Well Sort of . . . " Presentation to the Institute for International Research Quantitative Investment Management Seminar, October 1992.

Bernstein, Richard, "What's Going On? It's Earnings vs. Interest Rates," *Merrill Lynch Quantitative Viewpoint*, April 5, 1994.

Bernstein, Richard and Tew, Bernard, "The Equity Yield Curve," *Journal of Portfolio Management*, Fall 1991.

Fabozzi, Frank J. and Pollack, Irving M., *The Handbook of Fixed Income Securities* (Homewood, IL: Dow Jones-Irwin), 1983.

Leibowitz, Martin L., "Bond Equivalents of Stock Returns," *Journal of Portfolio Management*, Spring 1978, vol. 4, no. 3, pp. 25–30.

Leibowitz, Martin L., "Total Portfolio Duration: A New Perspective on Asset Allocation," *Financial Analysts Journal*, September/October 1986, vol. 42, no. 5, pp. 18–29, 77.

Leibowitz, Martin L., Sorenson, Eric, Arnott, Robert D., and Hanson, Nicholas, "A Total Differential Approach to Equity Duration," *Financial Analysts Journal*, September/October 1989, vol. 45, no. 5, pp. 30–37.

Leibowitz, Martin L. and Kogelman, Stanley, "Resolving the Equity Duration Paradox," *Financial Analysts Journal*, January/February 1993, pp. 51–64.

Ma, Christopher and Ellis, M. E., "Selecting Industries as Inflation Hedges," *Journal of Portfolio Management*, Summer 1989, pp. 45–48.

Macaulay, Frederick, *Some Theoretical Problems Suggested by the Movements of Interest Rates, Bond Yields, and Stock Prices in the United States since 1865* (New York: National Bureau of Economic Research), 1938.

Shiller, Robert J., *Market Volatility* (Cambridge, MA: The MIT Press), 1989.

Spiro, Peter S., "The Impact of Interest Rate Changes on Stock Price Volatility," *Journal of Portfolio Management*, Winter 1990, pp. 63–68.

8

Large vs. Small Stocks

*P*erhaps some of the best known studies of market segmentation are about company size. It appears today that even the casual investor is at least somewhat aware that smaller capitalization stocks have outperformed larger ones over the long term. Similarly, most investors are aware that the performance of smaller capitalization stocks, although superior over the long term, has historically demonstrated significant cycles of under- and outperformance. Despite that widespread acceptance, the *small stock effect* remains controversial, and some have suggested that the effect is merely a paper phenomenon that investors cannot actually attain in the real world (see, for example, Fouse (1989)). An important question that is not answered by the doubters of the small stock effect is why smaller capitalization stocks have had performance cycles at all. Achievable or not, the relationship between small stocks and large stocks is hardly stable, and style investors may be able to benefit greatly from a better understanding of what causes those cycles.

In addition, there are segments of small capitalization stocks that can be defined by some of the market segments outlined in earlier chapters. For example, there are small cap growth and small cap value stocks. The small stocks that comprise those market segments may be completely different in terms of fundamentals, of available Wall Street research coverage, and so forth and might perform quite differently through time. Their only commonality may be that they are all small stocks. The previously discussed issues of duration, neglect, valuation, expectations, and risk perception may influence the performance of smaller capitalization stocks.

This chapter will first review the concepts and definitions related to size investing. It will then investigate various market segments within the small cap universe, and some potential causes for the well-known cycles of small stock outperformance.

Figure 8.1 is the now familiar graph that shows the relative performance of the Ibbotson Small Stock Index versus the S&P 500. Based on the work of Ibbotson and Sinquefield (1976) and Banz (1981), investors began to understand that smaller capitalization stocks had historically provided excess returns above what could be explained by the Capital Asset Pricing Model (CAPM). It appeared that even when one accounted for the risk of smaller capitalization stocks (i.e., accounted for beta), small stocks provided superior returns.

One should note that Banz's work was published in 1981, and that smaller stock performance peaked in 1983. As small stocks underperformed during the 1980s, some skeptics began to point out that the market may have arbitraged away the small cap effect

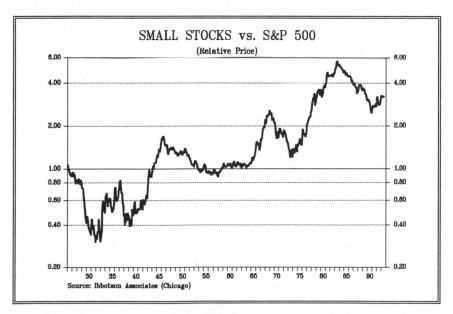

Figure 8.1 Small Stocks vs. S&P 500

once the effect was discovered and accepted. In other words, small stock outperformance was a function of no one knowing that smaller stocks were outperforming. Although that thought fits well into this book's Life Cycle concept, smaller stocks' underperformance during the 1980s can probably be explained by fundamental events. Nevertheless, their 1983 peak did indeed coincide with tremendous acceptance of small stock investing, and probably did indeed signal future underperformance similar to the acceptance that beta was dead during the early 1990s, roughly coinciding with higher beta stocks' once again beginning to outperform.

A dollar invested in the Ibbotson Small Stock Index in 1926 would have been worth about $2,757 by the end of 1993, while the same dollar invested in the S&P 500 would have been worth $800. Obviously, those figures are skewed, somewhat by the stock market crash of 1929, the subsequent bear markets of the 1930s, and the length of time shown in the graph. However, as Table 8.1 demonstrates, the historical probability of smaller stocks outperforming larger ones is relatively high as one's time horizon lengthened regardless of when one would have invested. The table shows the percent of the historical 6-, 12-, 36-, 60-, and 120-month holding period returns during which smaller stocks outperformed larger ones from 1926 to 1993.

Table 8.1 Historical Probability of Small Stocks Outperforming Large Stocks

Length of Holding Period	% Small Outperformed Large
6 Months	51.5%
12 Months	53.9%
36 Months	52.3%
60 Months	54.9%
120 Months	70.0%

NOTE: The table shows the percentage of the historical holding period returns from 1926 to 1993 during which smaller capitalization stocks outperformed larger capitalization stocks. The analysis is based on rolling holding period returns from monthly observations.

The performance cycles of smaller capitalization stocks cannot be ignored, however. If one had invested in smaller capitalization stocks when smaller cap stocks were at a relative performance peak, then it would have taken some time before a dollar invested in a small stock buy-and-hold strategy would have been worth the same as a dollar invested in a similar S&P 500 strategy. Table 8.2 shows the number of years that it would have taken for a small stock buy-and-hold strategy to return to the same dollar value as a similar S&P 500 strategy if the two strategies were initiated at various small stock relative performance peaks. Investing in small stocks at their relative performance peak has historically had tremendous opportunity costs because of the number of years it has usually taken for the two strategies to be *return neutral* (that is, in retrospect, an investor might have been neutral regarding the two strategies because the investments' values would be identical).

The table points out that the idea that smaller capitalization stocks outperform over the long-term may be somewhat misleading. Although they do indeed outperform point-to-point, 1926 to 1993, it has historically been extremely important for investors to be able identify when smaller capitalization stocks are near their relative performance peaks and troughs. Otherwise, one might have been constantly trying to catch up to the value of a large stock investment.

There are many ways to define small stocks, but most investors tend to focus on a stock's market capitalization (price times shares outstanding). One could use size of sales or revenues, total assets,

Table 8.2 Number of Years Until "Return Neutrality":
Small Stocks vs. S&P 500 When Investing at
Small Stock Relative Performance Peak

Small Stock Rel. Perf. Peak	Approx. Yrs. to "Return Neutrality"
1926	18
1937	6
1947	21
1969	9
1983	?

or number of employees, but most institutional investors prefer to use market capitalization because it is a traditional proxy for a stock's trading liquidity. A company's sales or total assets might be quite large, but if its nominal profits growth is poor, then the stock's price and its market value might be quite small. If market value is small, then trading becomes more difficult and, as a result, institutional investors prefer to define size according to market value. However, Figures 8.2 and 8.3 show the relationship between market value and sales and market value and number of employees, and the scatter diagrams suggest that one could probably use several definitions of size and not be overly concerned about trading liquidity.

Perold (1988) and Perold and Sirri (1994) have suggested that a portfolio's total transaction costs are a combination of commissions, taxes, market impact, and opportunity cost. While commissions and taxes are easily measured, market impact and opportunity cost are more difficult to quantify. Market impact is the movement in a stock's price that results from a trade that is too large given the stock's normal trading volume. An overly large buy or sell order disrupts the normal market process, bid/ask spreads widen, and

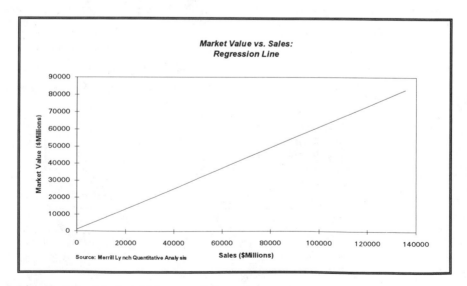

Figure 8.2 Market Value vs. Sales

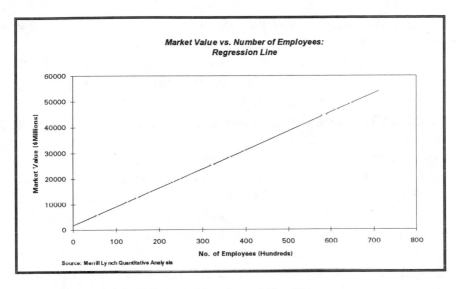

Figure 8.3 Market Value vs. Number of Employees

portfolio managers' performance results are penalized because they must buy at a higher price or sell at a lower price. Opportunity cost is the hidden transaction cost of not getting a trade completed within the portfolio manager's time frame. For example, suppose a manager wanted to buy 10,000 shares of a stock, but it normally traded only 1,000 shares per day. Ignoring that the portfolio manager's trader could buy the stock more quickly and incur higher market impact costs, or could ask a broker to risk capital and complete the trade immediately at a specific price, it might take ten days to complete the trade. However, the stock might appreciate during those ten days because of fundamental events. The performance lost over that ten-day period during which the 10,000 share position was not filled is called the opportunity cost. Because smaller capitalization stocks trade less frequently and in smaller amounts than do larger ones, small stock investors must always be aware of both the market impact and opportunity costs of their trades.

An intuitive method for determining a stock's trading liquidity has been proposed by Barth (1994), and suggests measuring a stock's liquidity by the number of days of historical dollar volume it would take to trade a million dollars of a stock. Dollar volume is simply the number of shares traded, multiplied by the price at which they traded during a given time period. Figure 8.4 shows the average number of days to trade a million dollars for stocks categorized by market capitalization based on trading and pricing data from February 1993 to February 1994. The data was limited to stocks on the NYSE and AMEX because NASDAQ trading data tends to double the actual number of shares traded. (That occurs because each of the two market makers involved in a NASDAQ transaction are credited with the trade and, thus, although 100 shares may be traded between market maker one and market maker two, 200 shares are recorded. That does not occur on the listed exchanges because there is only one specialist.) Figure 8.4 shows that $1 million dollar trades are easily transacted for most stocks, but that the time it might actually take to complete the trade goes up as market capitalization goes down. It might take nearly two full days, on average, to complete a $1 million dollar trade for a stock within the smallest market capitalization group, those with market capitalization below $250 million. For individual small

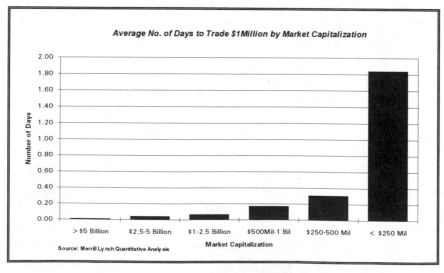

Figure 8.4   Days to Trade $1 Million by Market Capitalization

stocks, the "days-to-trade-a-million" measure can sometimes be well more than a week.

One study by Pradhuman and Bernstein (1994a) showed historical performance differentials by market capitalization. In that study, a universe of approximately six thousand stocks was broken into quarters by market capitalization and rebalanced annually from 1974 to 1993. The historical risk and return characteristics of each quarter were studied, and Table 8.3 summarizes the results of that risk/return analysis.

Although risk does increase as returns rise, the best Sharpe Ratio, or ratio of return to risk, was found among Mid-Cap stocks. That may be important for institutional investors because Mid-Cap stocks offer incremental small stock exposure (e.g., smaller although not small) and adequate trading liquidity. If Fouse was correct in the article cited earlier that any potential small stock effect might be negated by higher transaction costs, then the Mid-Cap universe may be the applicable small stock universe for institutional investors. They appear to offer more return per unit of risk, yet may not have the high transaction costs often associated with smaller capitalization stocks.

When investors refer to small cap investing, they often refer to investing in the stocks of relatively new companies that have some proprietary product or technology, and whose stocks are the result of recent public offerings. Those stocks usually sell at very high valuation multiples versus sales, book values, earnings and

Table 8.3 Risk/Return Characteristics by Market Capitalization (1974 to 1993)

Size	Annualized Return	Std. Deviation	Sharpe Ratio(*)
Large Stocks	11.0%	15.9%	.691
Mid-Cap Stocks	14.3%	17.3%	.827
Small Stocks	15.4%	19.1%	.806
Micro-Cap Stocks**	19.0%	23.4%	.812

(*) The Sharpe Ratio is the return divided by the standard deviation, or the return per unit of risk.
(**) The universe that comprises the Micro-Cap Stocks is the closest to that used within the Ibbotson Small Stock Index.
Source: Merrill Lynch Quantitative Analysis

cash flows, and are often called *emerging growth* stocks. Successful emerging growth stock managers, similar to all successful growth managers according to the Earnings Expectations Life Cycle framework, are successful because they are contrarian sellers. Proprietary products invite competition. The successful emerging growth manager identifies that competition, judges its strength, compares stock valuations, and decides when to sell. Thus, the successful emerging growth manager is often selling into strength.

Although emerging growth investing is probably the common vision of small company investing, those investment strategies examine only a portion of the total small stock universe. The other type of small cap stocks are more mature companies that used to have larger market capitalizations, and are generally not considered "sexy" or exciting. In other words, they are older, more mature companies that become smaller because of cyclical or secular periods of stock underperformance. That underperformance may have occurred because of product obsolescence or because of a recession. Those stocks are generally referred to as *small cap value* stocks. The key to success for the small cap value manager is to identify when these formerly large companies have reached their smallest market capitalizations.

This book has tried to dispel several generally accepted ideas of style investing, and the general impression of small stock investing appears to be centered on a major misconception. Figure 8.1, which demonstrated that small capitalization stocks outperform though time, is often used to support investing in emerging growth stocks. Unfortunately, that index is primarily based on small capitalization value issues. Morningstar, Inc., an examiner of mutual funds, appears to agree with that contention. Dimensional Fund Advisors (DFA) is a mutual fund company that offers an index fund that mirrors the performance of the Ibbotson Small Stock Index shown in that figure. Morningstar classifies that DFA fund as a small capitalization value fund because the stocks contained in the universe sell at very depressed levels to earnings and cash flows. Thus, it is ironic that many emerging growth managers justify investing in small cap stocks using the Ibbotson data, but that the mutual fund that attempts to mimic the performance of the

Ibbotson Index is classified as a small cap value fund. The entire small cap effect that is so often discussed may actually be a small capitalization value effect.

There are several ways to show the influence of small capitalization value stocks on the overall small cap universe. Because small capitalization value stocks can be characterized as older companies that have fallen on harder times, it follows that such stocks should have lower S&P Common Stock Ratings. Remember, those ratings are based on the stability and growth in earnings and dividends over a ten-year period. Companies that have had problems generally do not tend to have growth, let alone stability, in their earnings and dividends. Thus, the presence of a lower-quality bias within a smaller capitalization universe would tend to indicate the influence of smaller capitalization value stocks. Emerging growth stocks are more likely to be categorized as "not rated" because they are relatively new issues, and do not have the requisite ten years of historical earnings and dividends necessary to obtain an S&P Common Stock Rating.

Figure 8.5 shows the composition by Standard & Poor's Common Stock Ratings of the stocks within the Merrill Lynch Research

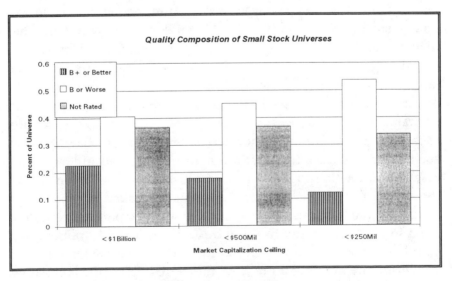

Figure 8.5 Quality Composition of Small Stock Universes

Universe (approximately 1,500 stocks) with market capitalizations below $1 billion dollars (750 stocks), below $500 million (485 stocks), and below $250 million (279 stocks). Regardless of the cutoff, lower-quality stocks, those rated B or worse, are the largest component of the small stock universe studied. Approximately 43 percent of the universe of stocks with market capitalizations below $1 billion dollars, 47 percent of those with market capitalizations below $500 million, and 57 percent of those with market capital- izations below $250 million are rated B or worse by S&P. The portion of a defined small stock universe that is comprised of lower- quality companies appears to grow as one lowers the market cap- italization ceiling used to define the universe. The center set of bars within the graph are those representing the proportion of each small stock universe that is rated B or worse. Note that the bars increase as the market cap ceiling decreases.

The average market capitalization of a C or D stock within that 1,500 stock universe is about $670 million, while the average market capitalization of a "not rated" stock is about $1.7 billion. One might think that averages might be misleading because of the influences of extreme values. However, using medians instead of averages does not alter the story. The median market capitalization among C and D stocks is only about $190 million, while the median among stocks without ratings is $575 million. Thus, while the me- dian market capitalizations of the two groups are indeed lower than the averages, the median "not rated" is still about three times as large as the median C and D company.

Smaller companies within the S&P 500 are generally small capitalization value stocks. In determining which stocks are added to the S&P 500 universe, Standard & Poor's looks for characteristics such as trading liquidity, institutional interest, and industry rep- resentation relative to the existing industry representation within the index. They tend to avoid new issues because it is harder to determine the long-term viability of a newer company (they do not want to add a company to the index only to have to remove it a year later because it went bankrupt), and because new issues tend to concentrate in popular or "hot" industries. Thus, the companies that tend to be added to the S&P 500 are usually not smaller capitalization stocks. Small stocks within the S&P 500 are solely those that were previously larger stocks.

Figures 8.6 and 8.7 show the relative performance of the fifty smallest stocks by market capitalization within the S&P 500 versus the equal-weighted S&P 500, and the quality composition of that fifty-stock portfolio. The portfolio has generally been outperforming the overall S&P 500 since late 1990, and 70 percent of the portfolio is rated B or worse by Standard & Poor's. That group's market capitalization ceiling is about $850 million, yet it has a considerably larger exposure to low-quality stocks than does the earlier full universe comprised of stocks with a market capitalization ceiling of only $250 million. That occurs because of the value characteristics of the smaller capitalization stocks within the S&P 500. These stocks are small only because they used to be large, and it is not uncommon for such stocks to have lost more than 75 percent of their peak market valuations.

Pradhuman and Bernstein (1994b) pointed out that smaller stock universes are currently dominated by stocks in industrial sectors. They found that stocks in the smaller capitalization quarters

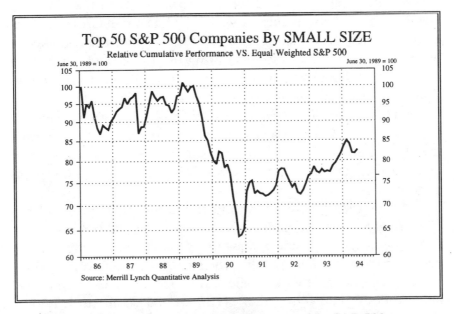

Figure 8.6 Performance of Small Stocks within the S&P 500

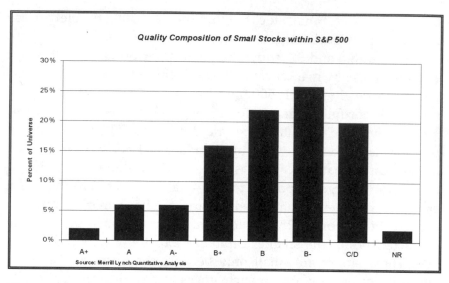

Figure 8.7   Quality Composition of S&P 500 Small Stock Portfolio

of the six-thousand stock universe previously mentioned, namely Mid-Cap, Small-Cap and Micro-Cap stocks, were overweighted in cyclical and capital spending sectors at year-end 1993, and underweighted in defensive sectors such as Consumer Growth, Consumer Staples, and Utilities. That finding makes sense given the outperformance of those sectors during the 1980s, and the relative growth in their market capitalizations. They defined cyclicals as Credit Cyclicals, Consumer Cyclicals, and Basic Industrials, and defined capital spending sectors as Capital Goods, Technology, and Conglomerates. Given that the historical earnings of those industries have historically displayed considerable volatility, it is likely that the average S&P common stock rating within that universe is quite low.

Another study supporting the contention that the small cap effect might be heavily influenced by small cap value stocks is by Fama, French, Booth, and Sinquefield (1993). They compared the performance of smaller capitalization stocks that traded on the New York Stock Exchange with smaller capitalization stocks that traded on NASDAQ, and found that NYSE-related small stock returns were significantly higher than NASDAQ-related small stock returns. Their conclusion was that the outperformance of NYSE small stocks was attributable to those companies' higher levels of distress; smaller NYSE companies tended to have poorer earnings histories and lower price/book value ratios than did NASDAQ small companies. In other words, NYSE small companies tended to fit the small cap value classification, while NASDAQ small companies tended to be emerging growth. The Ibbotson Small Stock Index was originally constructed using the ninth and tenth deciles of NYSE stocks classified by market capitalization. The preceding study, focusing on the performance differentials between NYSE and NASDAQ small stocks, thus supports the contention that the overall small stock effect may be a small cap value effect, and not necessarily related to emerging growth.

If the small stock effect is more of a small cap value effect than an emerging growth effect, and small cap value stocks tend to be lower-quality companies, then it might follow that the cycles of small stock out- and underperformance might be influenced by levels of nominal growth within the economy, similar to the relationships between growth and value and high- and low-quality stocks. Following the reasoning from earlier chapters regarding nominal growth and style performance, it would follow that smaller capitalization stocks would tend to outperform larger capitalization stocks when nominal growth rates within the economy increased, and would underperform when nominal growth rates decreased.

Figure 8.8 is a simple representation of the relationship between the small cap effect and nominal growth. As stated earlier, nominal growth rates within the economy have historically been greatly influenced by inflation, and the figure shows the relationship between the performance of the Ibbotson Small Stock Index relative to the S&P 500 and *secular inflation*. Secular inflation is defined as the five-year moving average of the year-to-year percent change in the Consumer Price Index (CPI). Secular inflation was used instead of actual inflation to smooth out short-term volatility in inflation, and to better identify the underlying inflation trend. Smaller capitalization stocks tend to outperform as secular inflation rises, and tend to underperform as secular inflation falls. If the earlier contention regarding the performance of lower-quality

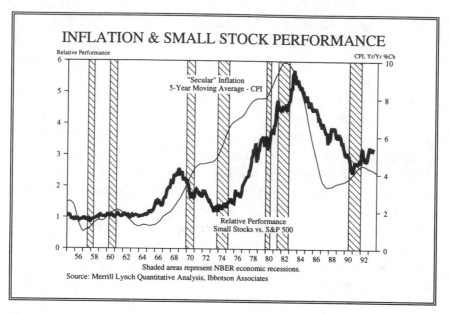

Figure 8.8 Small Stock Relative Performance and Secular Inflation

stocks and nominal growth is correct, then it follows that inflation, as a component of nominal growth, might be a strong stimulus for small stock outperformance.

One might ask why smaller stocks outperformed during the early 1990s because that period was essentially devoid of any meaningful inflation. As mentioned, nominal growth is composed of combinations of real growth and inflation, with rates of productivity within the economy generally determining the mix. Productivity improved significantly during the early 1990s and, thus, although inflation was low, smaller capitalization stocks outperformed in anticipation of increases in overall nominal growth. The unusual combination of small stock outperformance without inflation may have occurred because nominal growth rates, somewhat atypically, increased without inflation.

Figure 8.9 shows how improved productivity was within the U.S. economy during the 1990s by looking at rates of change in output per labor-hour within the nonfarm business sector (a traditional measure of productivity).

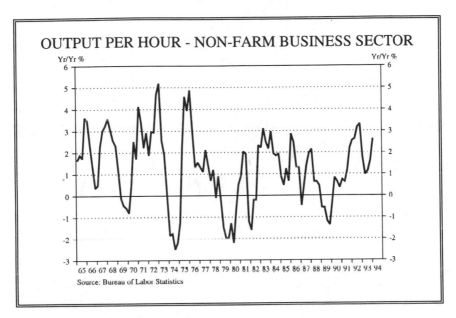

Figure 8.9 U.S. Productivity Levels

Pradhuman and Bernstein (1994c) examined the relationship between small stock performance and several economic and financial variables. They found that industrial production, inflation, and bond quality spreads were meaningful explanatory variables for the relative performance between small and large stocks between 1982 and 1993. Small stocks tended to outperform larger ones during periods of rising inflation and rising industrial production and when bond quality spreads were narrowing, and they attributed those results to the overall economic sensitivity of smaller capitalization stocks. Rising rates of industrial production and inflation obviously tend to correlate positively with nominal growth, and narrower quality spreads may reflect investors' willingness to accept the risk of more economically sensitive investments.

Figure 8.10 shows the inverse relationship between bond quality spreads and small stock relative performance. Smaller capitalization stocks tend to outperform larger ones as quality spreads narrow, and tend to underperform as quality spreads widen. Bond quality spreads tend to widen when investors become more skeptical about the economy, future nominal growth, and the ability of

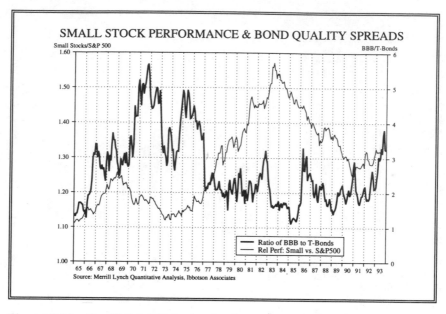

Figure 8.10   Small Stock Relative Performance and Bond Quality Spreads

the marginal company to survive. Because of those concerns, they tend to shift investments from riskier, lower-quality bonds to higher-quality corporate bonds or government T-Bonds. The yield spread widens because that shift in investor willingness to accept risk causes the prices of lower-quality bonds to fall relative to the prices of higher quality bonds. The inverse relationship between smaller capitalization stocks and bond quality spreads suggests that investors will not only shift away from lower-quality bonds when they believe that future nominal growth rates will weaken, but will also shift away from lower-quality stocks as well.

That inverse relationship between bond quality spreads and small stock relative performance suggests that investors make a rational choice between risky and less risky assets, and that investors must be enticed to hold assets that are perceived to be riskier. If safer, larger capitalization stocks offer similar growth and performance potential as do small stocks, then investors will gravitate toward safer stocks. They will be willing to hold riskier, smaller stocks only when they anticipate that those stocks will indeed provide superior growth and performance. If all things are equal between large and small stocks, then investors will probably prefer to hold larger stocks.

The risk/return relationships presented in each of the preceding chapters may help to explain investors' risk perceptions and their willingness to hold smaller capitalization stocks. The work presented on the relationship between growth and value, high and low quality, high and low beta, and long and short duration has attempted to demonstrate that investors become more willing to hold assets that are perceived to be riskier when they perceive that nominal growth rates will improve. Each of the concepts in the previous chapters can be used to help explain the performance cycles of smaller capitalization stocks.

For example, the equity yield curve, introduced in Chapter 7 on equity duration, attempts to gauge the risk/return tradeoff within the equity market between growth and duration risk. If expected growth rates are similar across the risk spectrum, then investors will tend to hold the least risky asset that offers that growth rate. If there is no incentive to take additional risk, e.g., if growth rates do not increase as risk increases, then investors will gravitate toward safe assets.

Bernstein and Tew (1991) suggested that the slope of the equity yield curve may be an indication of whether investors will be willing to accept the additional risk of smaller capitalization stocks. If the equity yield curve sloped upward, they suggested, it indicated that growth rates were indeed higher for longer duration equities. They felt that smaller capitalization stocks generally had lower dividend yields and, therefore, longer durations. Thus, if growth rates among longer-duration equities were higher than those of shorter-duration equities, then investors might be more willing to gravitate outward on the curve, and smaller capitalization stocks might outperform. However, if the curve was flat, and there was no risk premium attached to holding smaller capitalization stocks, then investors might not hold smaller companies. Bernstein and Tew showed that the equity yield curve was not only flat during parts of the 1980s, but also very high. With such a curve, investors were being offered significant amounts of growth among shorter-duration assets.

Many factors can affect investors' overall perceptions regarding the risk/return benefits or shortfalls incorporated into a small stock portfolio. Bernstein and Clough (1989) suggested that changes in the capital gains tax rate may have historically influenced the perceived risk/return tradeoff associated with smaller capitalization stocks. As mentioned, smaller capitalization stocks tend not to pay dividends, and investors must rely on capital gains as their sole source of return. An increase in the capital gains tax rate, therefore, would alter the after-tax expected returns of smaller capitalization stocks available to taxable investors. Bernstein found that smaller stocks (as defined by Ibbotson) tended to outperform larger ones when the capital gains tax rate was decreased, and that they underperformed when the tax rate increased.

Figure 8.11 shows the relationship between the performance of smaller capitalization stocks relative to that of the S&P 500 plotted against a blended capital gains tax rate. Smaller stocks have indeed tended to outperform larger ones as that tax rate has declined, and underperformed as the rate increased.

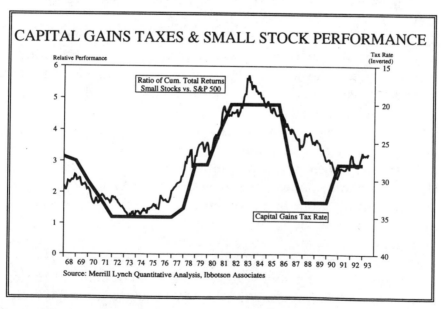

Figure 8.11 Small Stock Relative Performance and the Capital Gains Tax Rate

The equity yield curve analysis may further explain the effect that changes in the capital gains tax rate might have on risk/return relationships within the equity market. The after-tax equity yield curve will tend to flatten as the capital gains tax rate increases. An increase in the capital gains tax rate would probably decrease the expected returns of capital gains–oriented longer-duration assets more than those of shorter-duration assets and, because smaller stocks tend to be longer-duration assets, would decrease the relative attractiveness of smaller capitalization stocks.

The available information regarding a smaller capitalization company is generally less than that of a larger one, and smaller capitalization investors may be able to take advantage of that information asymmetry. The "neglected" stock effect was mentioned earlier, and pointed out that stocks that tended to be underfollowed by Wall Street analysts tend to outperform through time. It has been suggested that the lack of fundamental research may help explain the small stock effect. Figure 8.12 shows the relationship between market capitalization of S&P 500 stocks and the average number of analysts following them.

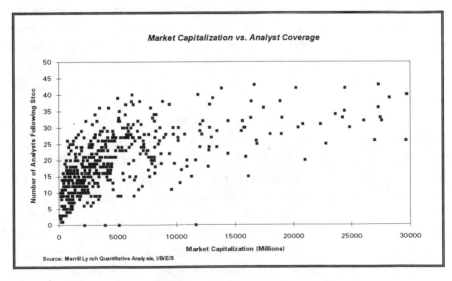

Figure 8.12 Market Capitalization vs. Analyst Coverage

Pradhuman and Bernstein (1994a) pointed out that an earnings surprise strategy, which attempted to predict earnings surprises, appeared to work better as the size of the company studied got smaller. They compared the performance strategies that concentrated on S&P 500 stocks, on Mid-Cap stocks, and on Small stocks, and found that the positive surprise model's predictive ability improved as market capitalization decreased. Although equal-weighted positive surprise portfolios of their S&P 500 version of the model outperformed the equal-weighted S&P 500 over an eight-year period, positive surprise portfolios constructed using their Mid-Cap version outperformed those of the S&P 500 version, and those constructed using the Small-Cap version outperformed those of the Mid-Cap version. They found similar results among S&P 500 and Mid-Cap negative surprise portfolios (Mid-Cap underperformed S&P 500), but found that the Small-Cap negative portfolio actually outperformed the market. They hypothesized that the negative surprise small stock portfolio performed so well because of their reliance on data from research analysts to predict earnings surprises, and the limitations of Wall Street research (Wall Street tends not to follow small, "bad" companies because they are hard to sell). In general, they felt that the information asymmetry was the reason that correct prediction of earnings surprises was more powerful as market capitalization decreased. In other words, if twenty analysts are following a stock, how much value can the twenty-first analyst add? However, if only four analysts are following a stock, then the fifth may have a higher probability of uncovering something the other four have not.

Because smaller capitalization stocks' businesses often cater to a local economy, the performance of smaller capitalization stocks is often influenced by the health of that local economy. The business conditions of a large firm that may operate worldwide are affected by variables that relate to the national or global economy. Smaller companies on the other hand tend to have operations that are less geographically diverse, and if a regional economy declines, then the business of the small companies within that economy might suffer more than the larger companies that have operations within that same region.

162

Bernstein and Clough (1990) found that smaller capitalization stocks behaved differently when classified by regions of the United States. Using a universe of more than five hundred companies with market capitalizations between $100 million and $400 million, they formed eight regional indices, and examined the risk/return relationships of those indices from 1985 to 1990. Table 8.4 summarizes the results of that study by showing the average quarterly price return of each index and each index's standard deviation of those quarterly returns. In addition, the table shows the correlations and betas between each index and the NASDAQ Composite.

There are considerable differences between the performance characteristics by regions. For example, the index based on stocks in the Southwest is by far the worst performing index, returning about 5 percent less per quarter than the Northwest index, reflecting that region's economic woes that resulted from the decline in oil prices during the period studied. The New England index similarly performed poorly reflecting the poor New England economy during the late 1980s.

Bernstein (1993) suggested that non-U.S. investors interested in investing in the United States to gain international diversification should do so by investing in smaller U.S. stocks rather than in the larger, better known issues to which foreign investors are often

Table 8.4   Risk/Return Analysis of Regional Small Stock Indices (1985–1990)

Region	Avg. Qtrly Ret.	Std. Deviation	NASDAQ Corr.	NASDAQ β
Northwest	4.5%	11.8%	0.88	0.93
Plains	4.1%	9.7%	0.94	0.83
South	3.2%	10.9%	0.98	0.97
Mid-Atlantic	3.0%	10.5%	0.96	0.92
West	2.8%	11.2%	0.97	0.99
Mid-West	2.5%	8.0%	0.95	0.68
New England	1.5%	10.8%	0.92	0.90
Southwest	−0.5%	9.8%	0.73	0.65
NASDAQ	3.7%	11.0%	1.00	1.00

Source: Merrill Lynch Quantitative Analysis

attracted. The study concluded that smaller U.S. stocks are more dependent on local economies, while larger U.S. stocks received a considerable proportion of their sales from outside the U.S. At the time, more than 22 percent of the sales of the S&P 500 came from abroad. Thus, adverse events outside the U.S. might affect not only non-U.S. financial markets, but also the sales and, in turn, the investment returns of larger U.S. stocks. Because of their lack of foreign exposure, U.S. small stocks are generally shielded from adverse events outside the U.S. Therefore, U.S. small stocks tend to provide better diversification for non-U.S. portfolios.

It was found that hypothetical combinations of international portfolios, defined by the MSCI-EAFE Index, and large U.S. stocks provided inferior risk/return combinations when compared to combinations of international portfolios and U.S. small stocks. It appears as though non-U.S. investors remove a major source of international diversification by demanding stock name familiarity in the U.S. stock market. Although not studied, it probably is true in reverse, and U.S. investors probably give up a large source of diversification by not investing in smaller non-U.S. stocks.

◈ Summary

♦ The performance differential between large and small capitalization stocks is perhaps the best known indication of market segmentation; however, its viability is not universally accepted.

♦ Nonetheless, it is important for style investors to understand the types of factors that influence the historical performance cycles between large and small stocks. Even if the so-called small stock effect is not attainable, style investors can tilt their portfolio toward smaller stocks to gain marginal advantage.

♦ Although smaller capitalization stocks do indeed outperform larger ones through time, investing at smaller capitalization relative performance peaks would have often been an inferior long term strategy.

♦ Investors tend to define size according to market capitalization because they believe that market capitalization is an indicator of trading liquidity. However, several other size variables, such as sales or number of employees, correlate well with market capitalization.

♦ Smaller capitalization stocks do tend to have higher transaction costs. One of the criticisms of the so called small cap effect is that it only works on paper, and that one could never trade the stocks in the real world and realize the performance idealized by the overall effect.

♦ Risk, as defined as the volatility of historical returns, does tend to increase as market capitalization decreases, but it appears as though Mid-Cap stocks have historically had higher returns per unit of risk than other market capitalization segments.

♦ Emerging growth stocks and small cap value stocks, although both small, perform quite differently.

♦ The small cap effect may actually be a small cap value effect, although it is often used incorrectly to support emerging growth investing.

♦ As with lower-quality and value investing, small stock investing has historically correlated with levels of nominal growth within the economy. Small stock performance has historically been influenced by such variables as inflation and productivity.

♦ The outperformance of smaller capitalization stocks reflects investors' willingness to accept additional risk. If there is no risk premium associated with investing in smaller capitalization stocks, then investors will gravitate toward larger capitalization stocks. The shape and slope of the equity yield curve represents those risk/return tradeoffs.

◆ The capital gains tax rate tends to affect the after-tax expected returns of smaller capitalization stocks more than those of larger ones because smaller stocks do not tend to pay dividends.

◆ There is an information asymmetry between small and large stocks because a smaller number of analysts tend to follow the average small stock. That lack of information flow might cause the insightful investor to be additionally rewarded.

◆ Smaller capitalization stocks may be more influenced by the health of local economies rather than by the health of the national or global economy. Because of that, small stock performance by region of the United States can vary greatly.

◆ Small stocks may provide superior diversification benefits to non-U.S. investors than can large U.S. stocks. International investors may remove a major source of diversification by demanding name familiarity when investing in the U.S. market.

◆ References

Banz, Rolf W. "The Relationship Between Return and Market Value of Common Stocks." *Journal of Financial Economics*, 1981, vol. 9, no. 1, pp. 3–18.

Barth, Markus. "New Liquidity Analysis Method: Days to Trade a Million." Merrill Lynch Quantitative & Convertible Research internal memo, January 1994.

Bernstein, Richard and Clough, Jr., Charles I. "The Capital Gains Tax Rate." *Merrill Lynch Quantitative Viewpoint*, August 1, 1989.

Bernstein, Richard. "Small Stock Performance and Investor Risk Perception." Second Annual Symposium on Small Firm Financial Research, April 1990.

Bernstein, Richard. "Taxes Transform An Ugly Duckling." *Institutional Investor Middle Markets Forum*, vol. XXIV, no. 14, October 1990.

Bernstein, Richard. "U.S. Small Stocks for Non-U.S. Investors." *Merrill Lynch Equity Derivatives Update*, October 27, 1993.

Bernstein, Richard, and Clough, Jr., Charles I. "Interregional Equity Portfolio Diversification." *Merrill Lynch Quantitative Viewpoint*, March 13, 1990.

Bernstein, Richard and Pradhuman, Satya D. "The Small Stock Effect: It May Be Value Not Growth." *Merrill Lynch Quantitative Viewpoint*, November 3, 1992.

Bernstein, Richard and Pradhuman, Satya D. "Emerging Growth and Interest Rates." *Merrill Lynch Equity Derivatives Strategy Update*, January 1, 1994.

Fouse, William. "The Small Stock Hoax." *Financial Analysts Journal*, July/August 1989, pp. 12–15.

Ibbotson, Roger G. and Sinquefield, Rex A. "Stocks, Bonds, Bills, and Inflation: Year-By-Year Historical Returns (1926–1974)." *Journal of Business*, 1976, vol. 49, no. 1, pp. 11–47.

Perold, Andre. "The Implementation Shortfall: Paper Versus Reality." *Journal of Portfolio Management*, Spring 1988.

Perold, Andre and Sirri, Erik H. "The Costs of International Trading." Working paper, Harvard Business School, April 1994.

Pradhuman, Satya D. and Bernstein, Richard. *Merrill Lynch Small Cap Perspective*, January 5, 1994.

Pradhuman, Satya D. and Bernstein, Richard. *Merrill Lynch Small Cap Perspective*, March 4, 1994.

Pradhuman, Satya D. and Bernstein, Richard. *Merrill Lynch Small Cap Perspective*, May 5, 1994.

PART III

9

Implications for
Plan Sponsors

*D*uring 1989 and 1990, there was considerable discussion both in the popular and financial press regarding the outstanding performance of growth managers and the significant underperformance of value managers. One article even went so far as to delve into a particular value manager's portfolio, and to discuss the number of clients that were dropping the manager because of poor performance. Such relative performance for a style-driven manager may be perfectly normal. As this book has tried to point out, the equity market goes through both secular and cyclical periods of style and market segment performance.

As the equity market goes through phases during which styles of investing go in and out of favor, plan sponsors may want to strategically or tactically reallocate funds among managers, or "tilt" their overall plan toward a particular equity style rather than go through the process of hiring and firing managers. Not only is the firing/hiring process costly and time-consuming, but because managers are usually fired with hindsight, it adds the potential risk of being out of step in terms of style with the overall equity market. A well-planned style allocation strategy and manager review process may significantly enhance the returns of the equity portion of the pension plan.

Plan sponsors must resist the temptation to simply look for the best performing manager, even on a risk-adjusted basis. The Earnings Expectations Life Cycle demonstrates that the popularity of a style and its subsequent success may be inverse. Thus, when a stock selection method, and therefore a manager who follows that particular method, becomes overwhelmingly popular, it may well be a sign of future underperformance. Table 9.1 examines the five best one-year performance periods for the growth and value manager performance indices highlighted earlier, and the subsequent one-year performance. Extraordinary one-year performance for a particular style is often followed by a period of underperformance.

Plan sponsors who had decided to hire a growth-oriented manager because of his or her outstanding one-year performance might have been rather disappointed in that growth manager's performance during the subsequent year after being hired. Value managers, as defined by the index used, outperformed growth managers subsequent to four of the five best years for growth managers, and did so by an average of about 350 basis points. Plan sponsors

Table 9.1 Five Best Performing Years by Style and Subsequent One-Year Performance

Year	Growth Perform-ance	Value Perform-ance	Subse-quent Year	Growth Perform-ance	Value Perform-ance
Best Growth					
1975	40.2%	39.5%	1976	24.0%	**37.5%**
1979	35.2%	25.5%	1980	**33.6%**	25.4%
1991	33.7%	23.8%	1992	4.9%	**11.1%**
1980	33.6%	25.4%	1981	2.5%	**5.8%**
1982	31.0%	23.8%	1983	23.7%	**26.2%**
Best Value					
1975	40.2%	39.5%	1976	24.0%	**37.5%**
1976	24.0%	37.5%	1977	**10.7%**	3.0%
1985	28.8%	29.1%	1986	16.5%	**19.1%**
1983	23.7%	26.2%	1984	0.5%	**7.5%**
1979	36.2%	25.5%	1980	**33.6%**	25.4%

Note: Performance is based on the annual total return performance of the Merrill Lynch Quantitative Analysis Growth and Value Fund Indices. Figures in **bold** in the last two columns highlight the superior performing style.
Source: Merrill Lynch Quantitative Analysis

who hired value managers after the value managers' best years had a slightly smaller chance of being disappointed. Value managers outperformed growth managers subsequent to three of the five best value manager years. (One should note though that growth managers actually outperformed value managers during two of the five best initial value years.) Thus, merely chasing performance and hiring/firing managers based on the performance of the overall style can result in inferior performance for the equity portion of the plan.

Pension consultants often suggest that plan sponsors examine risk-adjusted returns, rather than absolute returns, so Table 9.2 is similar to 9.1 except that it examines the five best performing years on a risk-adjusted basis. Risk-adjusted returns are calculated by dividing the annual total return of the particular index by the standard deviation (variability) of the monthly returns within a given

Table 9.2 Five Best Risk-Adjusted Performing Years and Subsequent One-Year Performance

Year	Growth Performance	Value Performance	Subsequent Year	Growth Performance	Value Performance
			Best Growth		
1989	27.6%	22.5%	1990	−2.9%	**−5.4%**
1985	28.8%	29.1%	1986	16.5%	**19.1%**
1983	23.7%	26.2%	1984	0.5%	**7.5%**
1975	40.2%	39.5%	1976	24.0%	**37.5%**
1991	33.7%	23.8%	1992	4.9%	**11.1%**
			Best Value		
1983	23.7%	26.2%	1984	0.5%	**7.5%**
1985	28.8%	29.1%	1986	16.5%	**19.1%**
1993	11.6%	14.7%	1994	?	?
1976	24.0%	37.5%	1977	**10.7%**	3.0%
1975	40.2%	39.5%	1976	24.0%	**37.5%**

Note: Performance is based on the annual total return performance of the Merrill Lynch Quantitative Analysis Growth and Value Fund Indices. Figures in **bold** in the last two columns highlight the superior performing style.
Source: Merrill Lynch Quantitative Analysis

year. Superior risk-adjusted returns can also be a style rotation trap, however, more so for growth-oriented investing than for value-oriented investing. The table's results show that outstanding risk-adjusted performance among growth funds was followed four out of five times by a year of absolute underperformance. For value funds, however, a year during which value funds had superior risk-adjusted returns to those of growth funds was only followed once by a year of underperformance. In a moment, we will investigate further the historical risk of growth and value investing.

Plan sponsors should establish an overall equity style strategy that both meets the liability needs of the pension plan and provides the superior risk/return potential necessary for long-term planning, rather than simply firing underperforming managers. Several points should be considered when establishing such strategies.

First, the plan sponsor should have a good historical perspective regarding style performance, and should understand how the macro- and microeconomic influences outlined in this book not only affect style performance, but more important, how they affect the sponsor company's ability to make plan contributions. Pensions assets should be diversified relative to the overall corporate assets to ensure survival of the pension plan should the company fail. It probably does not make sense for companies within more mature and cyclical industries, like steel or chemicals, to employ solely value managers, because the sales and profitability of those companies and, therefore, their abilities to make contributions to the pension plan would tend to deteriorate at the same time that value-oriented strategies would tend to underperform. Growth companies' pension plans should similarly limit their investment exposure to their own industries. Thus, although corporate failure may be an extreme case, diversification relative to corporate assets can greatly influence the funding status of the plan and the corporation's ability to make plan contributions.

Cynics would suggest that corporations have little incentive to follow that idea of diversification from corporate assets because of the Pension Benefit Guarantee Corporation (PBGC), a government-sponsored body that ensures that pensioners will be paid in the event of a corporate failure. They would suggest that the PBGC essentially writes a company a put option on the company's pension liabilities, which the company would exercise in the event of corporate failure. With that put protection, cynics could argue that companies couldn't care less about diversifying pension assets relative to corporate assets. On the other hand, however, one could argue that the put that the PBGC provides allows the plan sponsor the fortitude to take the additional risk sometimes necessary to ensure that the plan can meet its obligations. Either way, the concepts outlined in this chapter assume that the company is acting in good faith.

Public pension funds, contrary to popular political strategy, probably should minimize investment in their own municipalities. Public funds are sometimes politically encouraged to invest within their own municipalities in order to stimulate economic growth within the local area. Although on the surface that might seem to make sense, it is a classic case of "putting one's eggs all in one basket." As pointed out in Chapter 8, smaller companies tend to be influenced by their local economies, and small company stock price performance can vary greatly by region of the United States. If a state has a local recession, then the probability increases that intrastate smaller company investments will underperform. For example, a state whose economy is centered on oil production should attempt to avoid investing pension funds in oil-related industries. If the price of oil were to decline, then both the local economy and the state's pension assets would decline. At a time when tax revenues would most likely be declining because of falling personal and corporate incomes, the state's pensions assets would also be declining in value as well, thus potentially putting double the pressure on the state to be able to meet pension obligations. Investing large proportions of public pension assets within the municipality might be a short-term solution to economic woes, but it might also sacrifice the long-term growth of the overall public pension plan.

Second, it is important for plan sponsors to examine a manager's relative performance versus peers rather than absolute performance when choosing an equity style manager or when judging the performance of an existing manager. Even the worst manager following a particular style might perform well both absolutely and relative to a broad market benchmark like the S&P 500 when the manager's particular style is in favor. Plan sponsor/manager relationships are often simply based on the manager's performance relative to the S&P 500, and that may let inferior style managers hide their true lack of ability. Managers should be gauged against a representative peer group so that style managers who may outperform a broad market benchmark, yet are among the bottom half of their style peers, are not considered "good" managers.

Pension consultants tend to disagree with the notion that managers should be compared to their peers. Bailey (1992) suggests that there are several problems with peer group benchmarks, including survivorship bias ("bad" managers are dropped from the universe because they go out of business), conceptual shortcomings (do the managers in the sample consistently adhere to the particular style?), and a failure for most to pass benchmark "quality" tests. Note that both consultants and portfolio managers may have vested interests in plan sponsors *not* using peer group analysis. Consultants do not like peer group analysis because it lessens the importance of the consultant's role in the manager selection process. Portfolio managers do not like peer analysis because the managers may have marketing strategies in which they define investable universes for clients, only to find that those defined universes ended up underperforming, which in turn prevented the managers from outperforming the representative peer group. Nonetheless, the criticisms of peer relative performance are well taken because it is indeed difficult to gauge a manager's performance against an ever-changing universe of managers who are realistically not necessarily bound to follow their defined or stated style, which is to say, if growth was outperforming value, then it might be easy to find a value manager in growth manager's clothing. Even considering those problems, though, comparing a style manager to a representative peer group may be the only method for determining the manager's true skill.

A reasonable peer group method might be to rank all managers following a particular style according to performance relative to their individually prearranged customized benchmarks or normal portfolios. In other words, if value manager #1 was prevented from buying stocks that did not pay dividends, and value manager #2 was not so restricted, then #1 might be gauged against a benchmark comprised solely of dividend paying value stocks, while #2 might be judged against a broader value universe. If #1's absolute performance was −10 percent, but #1's benchmark declined by 15 percent, then #1 would have outperformed the benchmark by 500 basis points. If #2's absolute performance was 10 percent, but #2's benchmark appreciated 15 percent, then #2 would have underperformed the benchmark by 500 basis points. In the peer group ranking, #1 would be considered a better manager than #2. That method would allow portfolio managers to feel that they were being fairly judged against their competition, and plan sponsors would have a means of judging manager skill on a relative basis.

The cycles of style investing that have been described can put significant pressures on the business of style-oriented money management firms. As noted earlier, the underperformance of value managers during 1989–1990 is a recent example of those pressures. The asset bases of many value managers were reduced substantially during that time period both because of poor performance and because of pension accounts moving to other managers. Assets under management are critical to a money management firm's profitability and success as a business venture because most money managers derive their revenues based on a percent of assets under management. If total assets under management decline, then the firm's revenues will usually decline as well.

In order to smooth their revenue streams, traditional style managers may take several routes. The first, and most obvious, is to offer a broader range of investment funds. A traditional large capitalization value manager may begin to offer a small capitalization, value-oriented fund, or an emerging growth manager may offer a Mid-Cap or Large-Cap growth fund. In these examples, the money management firm has attempted to smooth the cyclical revenues that might be caused by cycles between large and small stocks' performance. More recently, some firms have begun to offer international investment products that promise to follow similar investment objectives to those the firm follows in its United States–oriented portfolios (international growth stocks, and so on) in order to take advantage of the relative outperformance of international markets that could ultimately boost the value of the firm's underlying assets under management.

Plan sponsors should be wary of new investment products from firms that have no demonstrated expertise in a particular market segment or style. There are plenty of money managers who have demonstrated expertise in nearly any investment style one could imagine. More important, the Earnings Expectations Life Cycle analogy suggests the outperformance of a particular style is more likely to soon end when firms that have steadfastly maintained one investment approach finally concede and begin to offer products that may be counter to the firms' traditional approach or area of expertise.

The cycles of style performance make it tempting for plan sponsors to actively asset allocate among style managers. As stated, some do without realizing that they do through the manager firing/ hiring process. A more beneficial approach may be to tactically or strategically reallocate funds among style mangers. (Chapter 10 will point out that the use of equity derivatives can help facilitate such reallocations, but for now the discussion will center on the cash equity market.) Pensions funds reallocate funds among stock and bond managers based on forecasts of expected returns and liability funding needs, but do not fire one set of managers because the asset class that they manage is expected to underperform. Plan sponsors do not tend to fire bond managers because bonds are expected to underperform stocks, so why should they not reallocate equity funds according to style expected returns and liability funding needs in a similar fashion to stock/bond allocation decisions?

Some plan sponsors are hesitant to attempt to actively predict style returns, although most corporations already have an infrastructure in place for doing so. The corporate economist is usually responsible for outlining the economic guidelines under which the company sets it strategic plans. That set of economic scenarios may provide the necessary information for anticipating style performance. If the economist or strategic planning group suggests that its forecasts of industrial production and nominal growth are becoming more optimistic, then the pension plan should shift toward value, Small-Cap, lower-quality, and higher beta stocks according to the ideas presented throughout this book. If its forecasts are becoming more pessimistic, then the plan should shift toward growth, Large-Cap, higher-quality, and lower beta stocks. Basically, if the strategic planning of the entire corporation is based on an economic forecast, and the firm risks its future on such forecasts, then that information should be certainly adequate for the implementation of basic style rotation by the managers of the pension plan.

A more recent alternative for plan sponsors who want to limit the performance swings of following one particular style is to hire a GARP manager. Growth at a reasonable price (GARP) is a more recent response by growth and value style managers to smooth the performance cycles affecting their business, and has been noted by Adam (1994) and others. GARP attempts to cross the growth/value borders by searching for growth stocks that appear undervalued, or undervalued stocks that have unappreciated growth potential. The growth in equity assets being managed by GARP management techniques may be the result of the leaders of the 1980s, namely large capitalization growth stocks, underperforming substantially through much of the early 1990s.

Within the context of the Earnings Expectations Life Cycle, successful GARP-oriented investment strategies would fall roughly at nine o'clock, or at the point where value meets growth. Of course, one would prefer to buy stocks at six o'clock, but that would probably be considered growth at a *cheap* price. The word reasonable implies that the growth has indeed been visible and begun to be recognized by equity market participants. While the traditional growth manager might simply look for the stocks with the highest potential growth, the GARP manager might buy stocks with a weaker absolute level of potential growth if those stocks are relatively cheaper. The GARP manager attempts to identify whether a company's growth that has already been identified is sustainable, and reasonably priced given that sustainability. One could argue that any growth manager should be a GARP manager (remember, good growth is from nine o'clock to midnight on the Life Cycle), but the coining of the phrase and GARP money management firms' recent marketing successes within the plan sponsor community suggest that plan sponsors feel that traditional growth managers do not pay attention to value, and may tend to buy stocks more toward midnight on the Life Cycle.

A traditional GARP-oriented strategy, although usually not referred to by that name, is P/E-to-growth rate. P/E-to-growth strategies, as their name implies, search for stocks whose ratio of P/E to projected earnings growth is relatively low. That implies that the stock may be relatively undervalued given its anticipated earnings growth potential. For example, suppose that one company's P/E ratio is ten times earnings, and analysts expect the company to grow at 10 percent per year for the next five years, and that a second company's P/E ratio is fifteen time earnings and its five-year projected earnings growth rate is similarly 10 percent per year. The first company would probably be more attractive to a GARP manager, assuming all other variables are identical for the two companies, because the P/E-to-growth rate for the first company is 1.0 (10 divided by 10), while that for the second company is 1.5 (15 divided by 10), and an investor would have to pay less for the same anticipated growth. Peters (1991, 1993) shows numerous tests of low P/E-to-growth strategies and their consistency of outperformance relative to a growth stock universe. He terms low P/E-to-growth a "contrarian approach to growth stock investing" because the P/E-to-growth rate investor is essentially looking for the out-of-favor stocks within the growth stock universe. Similarly, Durand (1992) demonstrates the need for determining how much to pay for a stock's growth potential, and how performance can be hurt simply by examining growth potential alone.

Currently, there may be two types of GARP-oriented managers, and plan sponsors need be wary of one of them. One type carefully selects stocks, often quantitatively, so as to be relatively neutral between a pure value or a pure growth exposure. Those managers may have any combination of stocks that appear on the left side of the Earnings Expectations Life Cycle, but the overall portfolio will average at roughly nine o'clock.

The second type of GARP manager is the growth or value manager who has been underperforming, and chases outperforming stocks that are not within the normal universe. Thus, they claim to be GARP managers because they are not able to find attractive investment ideas within their traditional universes of stocks. For example, an underperforming growth manager might start buying outperforming value stocks while claiming that they are the stocks that are truly growing; or a value manager might buy outperforming growth stocks while claiming that value is meaningless without profitability and stock performance. It appears as though relative strength and performance are the important stock selection characteristics for this type of GARP manager, rather than growth and value.

It is the latter group of which plan sponsors should be wary. The Life Cycle analogy suggests that managers who might violate their original disciplines probably do so just as their original discipline begins to once again perform well. Chasing after performance under the guise of a GARP discipline should suggest a lack of understanding of growth, of value, and of GARP itself.

Plan sponsors sometimes worry solely about the returns of the assets within their equity funds and the overall plan. But it is also important to consider the risk or volatility of the funds as well. The purpose of a pension plan is ultimately to pay benefits to retiring workers, and those payments are the plan's liabilities. It is the plan sponsor's responsibility to make sure that the assets of the plan are adequate at any point in time to match the liabilities that must be paid out. Thus, if the average age of the employees in the plan is relatively young, and the probability of cash outflow demands on the fund are relatively low, then the near-term volatility of the returns of the fund may be of less concern to the plan sponsor than it would to the manager of a plan whose participants' average age was much higher. Short-term underperformance that might occur as part of a longer-term strategy to gain higher returns for the overall plan would most likely be of little concern to the plan sponsor whose participant average age is young because the cash outflows from the fund may not occur for many years, and the risk of not having an adequate level of assets to meet liability demands (often called underfunding) is low. However, more mature plans may not be able to withstand short-term volatility because the risk of underfunding might be quite high. (There are many issues related to underfunding from a legal, ethical, accounting, and shareholder point of view, but they are beyond the scope of this book.)

Investors are, at one time or another, taught the relationship between risk and return. As pointed out in earlier chapters, generally risk and return go hand in hand, meaning that investors receive higher returns if they are willing to take more risk. That dichotomous relationship may present problems for the plan sponsor because all plan sponsors would like to receive the highest returns possible to reduce the risk of underfunding, but the plan sponsor must necessarily increase the risk of underfunding to gain those higher returns. Thus, plan sponsors must carefully determine the funding needs, and then assess the risk tolerance that the equity portion of the overall plan can tolerate. The plan that takes unnecessary risk to gain higher returns, or the plan that does not take enough risk can both quickly become underfunded.

Table 9.3, taken from Bernstein, Pradhuman, and Barth (1993a), shows the average twelve-month returns of various equity-oriented indices, as well as two measures of their risk. The first risk measure is the traditional standard deviation of those twelve-month returns. The standard deviation measures the volatility, and therefore the predictability, of returns. Less predictable returns are

Table 9.3 Equity Risk/Return Relationships
(1971 to September 1993)

Equity Index	Avg. 12-Month Total Ret.	Standard Deviation	% of Returns That Were Negative
S&P 500	13.3%	16.2%	20.9%
MLQA Value Fund Index	14.9%	14.2%	17.6%
MLQA Growth Fund Index	15.1%	19.5%	20.2%
MSCI-EAFE	16.3%	24.2%	25.6%
Ibbotson Small Stock Index	17.5%	24.4%	23.8%

Source: Merrill Lynch Quantitative Analysis, MSCI, S&P, Ibbotson Associates

considered more risky than are those that are more predictable. The second measure is the percent of the twelve-month periods in which the return was negative; in other words, the percent of time one would have lost money.

They examined the twelve-month total returns of four indices beside the S&P 500. The other four indices were:

1. *MLQA Value Fund Index*: A proprietary index of the total return of nine large growth and income mutual funds. This is an equal-weighted index, and is the total return version of the value fund index presented earlier in the book, and was used in Tables 9.1 and 9.2.

2. *MLQA Growth Fund Index*: A proprietary index of the total return of nine large growth mutual funds. This is an equal-weighted index, and is the total return version of the growth fund index presented earlier in the book, and was used in Tables 9.1 and 9.2.

3. *International Stocks*: The total returns of the Morgan Stanley Capital International (MSCI) Europe/Australia/Far East (EAFE) Index based in U.S. dollars.

4. *Small Stocks:* The returns of the Ibbotson Small Stock Index as calculated by Ibbotson Associates in Chicago. They define small stocks as the ninth and tenth deciles of the NYSE, plus any AMEX and OTC stocks that fit under that ceiling.

A simple example will quickly differentiate the two measures of risk. A classic question to ask regarding the risk and return of investments is which is the riskier asset: $100 in shares in a stock mutual fund or $100 of lottery tickets? Using standard deviation as the definition of risk, it turns out that the lottery tickets are the safer investment. One really does not know the investment outcome of the shares in the mutual fund because the stock market could go up or down by varying degrees. However, one can be relatively certain of the investment return from the lottery tickets: −$100. One should not confuse the range of potential outcomes with the certainty of those outcomes. The returns of the mutual fund through time are hopefully positive, but that positive return is uncertain. There is no virtually no uncertainty regarding the outcome of the lottery (someone else will win it!), and thus the lottery is the safer investment when one defines risk using standard deviation. If one were to use the percent of the returns that were negative, then the lottery quickly becomes the more risky invest- ment because, although the outcome is relatively certain, it will almost certainly be negative (losing all the money or -100 percent return). Thus, even if one got lucky and won the lottery once in a while, the probability of a negative return would still be quite high relative to that of the mutual fund.

In this example, and the ones that follow, the alternative mea- sure of risk is the percent of the returns that were less than 0, but plan sponsors could make that definition more meaningful by changing it to the percent of the returns that fell below some bench- mark or some historical or forecasted liability requirement. Re- cently, articles by Frank (1992), Harlow (1991), and Leibowitz, et al. (1992) examined definitions of risk that might be more realistic for the plan sponsor, and those risk definitions' implications for plan funding needs. For the purposes of this book, and in the interest of simplicity, the alternative definition of risk will be the percent of the returns that were negative.

In Table 9.3, one can see that risk and return do indeed tend to go together. The S&P 500 had the lowest 12-month average return, but also had a relatively low standard deviation and prob- ability of a negative return, while smaller capitalization stocks had the highest return, but also had among the highest standard de- viation and probability of a negative return. There do appear to be some inconsistencies, however. Note that the Value Funds have a higher return than did the S&P 500, but that their standard de- viation and probability of negative returns was lower than that of the S&P 500. Similarly, note that smaller capitalization stocks had higher returns than did international stocks, but had a lower prob- ability of negative returns.

Figure 9.1 represents the scatter diagram of historical risk/ return relationships using columns 2 and 4 from Table 9.3. The vertical axis measures the average twelve-month return from the

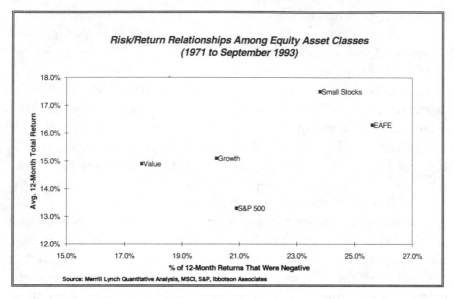

Figure 9.1   Risk/Return Relationships Among Equity Asset Classes

particular equity asset class over the twenty-three year period studied, and the horizontal axis represents the percent of the twelve-
month returns that were negative. In all such charts, the goal is to
attempt to invest in a portfolio that will end up northwest of the
other strategies. Portfolios lie northwest of each other when they
have experienced higher returns (north), but with less risk (west).

The results suggest that both value and growth managers have
been able to provide returns that were superior to those of the S&P
500 both on an absolute and a risk-adjusted basis. The authors
proposed that their findings questioned the worth of long-term S&P
500 indexing because both growth and value managers' historical
performance sit northwest of the S&P 500. (They did admit, however, that their universe of managers was biased toward successful
managers.) They further suggested, contrary to popular belief, that
value-oriented strategies may be more appropriate for long-term,
risk-averse investors. They pointed out that their universe of
growth managers outperformed their universe of value managers
by only twenty basis points per year, but that the value managers
had negative returns only 17.6 percent of the time, compared to

20.2 percent for the growth managers. Thus, a long-term commitment to a successful value manager may actually be more conservative than running an S&P 500 index fund.

Plan sponsors rarely commit their entire equity portion of the pension fund to a single equity strategy. Thus, it may be more important for the plan sponsor to examine combinations of equity assets rather than each asset alone. The intercorrelation, or lack thereof, between different types of equity strategies could potentially reduce the risk of the overall equity portion of the plan.

Smaller stocks and international stocks have attracted investor attention perhaps largely because of the higher returns that they have historically offered. As Table 9.3 highlights, small stocks as measured by the Ibbotson Small Stock Index have returned approximately 17.5 percent per year over the twenty-three year period studied, while the MSCI-EAFE index returned about 16.3 percent per year. Obviously, those historical returns compare quite well versus the S&P 500's 13.3 percent annualized return.

Perhaps a better rationale for investing in these two groups is the diversification that they offer rather than their past returns. Diversification is sometimes highlighted in terms of higher returns, but it is really a risk control concept. The goal of diversification probably should be to offset the adversity affecting one particular asset class with the returns of another asset class that are less affected or not affected at all by the adverse event. Better diversification can generally be achieved if the assets chosen have lower correlations of returns. Stocks within the same market may provide industry or sector diversification, but they will all generally still be affected by the movement of the overall market to which they all belong. On the other hand, stocks in a completely different market may provide more diversification because they may be further removed from the particular adversity. It should be pointed out they may be further removed from potential benefits as well.

While it is generally well known that international stocks provide significant diversification benefits to U.S. investors because non-U.S. stocks are less directly influenced by the U.S. economy, it appears to be less well known that non-U.S. investors have historically had the opportunity to receive similar diversification benefits from U.S. small stocks. Non-U.S. investors tend to buy S&P 500-type stocks because of their familiarity. However, they might improve returns, both on an absolute and risk-adjusted basis, by altering their focus toward the secondary U.S. equity market.

Figure 9.2 shows risk/return combinations (using the percent of the annual returns that were negative as the definition of risk rather than the traditional volatility of returns) between the S&P 500, small stocks and international stocks. One can see the traditional frontiers carved out by the various combinations, and that the frontiers are scalloped, rather than straight lines, because of the diversification effects between the assets. The curves will be more scalloped when the correlations between the assets are lower. The risk/return combinations between two assets that were perfectly correlated would be represented by a straight line.

The curve representing combinations of S&P 500 stocks and international stocks is more scalloped than the one representing combinations of S&P 500 and U.S. small stocks. That implies that large capitalization–oriented U.S. pension plans may find it more

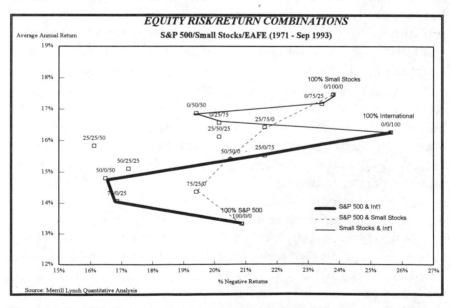

Figure 9.2 Risk/Return Combinations of Selected Equity Asset Groups

184

advantageous to diversify by investing abroad than by investing in the secondary markets.

The curve representing the combinations of small stocks and international stocks is more scalloped than the one representing combinations of S&P 500 and international stocks, and suggests that non U.S. pension plans have historically received both increased returns *and* decreased risk when adding even limited amounts of smaller capitalization U.S. stocks to their overall equity portfolios. For example, the point representing 75 percent international stocks and 25 percent U.S. small stocks (0/25/75) lies northwest of the portfolio that contained 75 percent international stocks and 25 percent S&P 500 (25/0/75).

This type of risk/return analysis usually incorporates one-year time horizons. However, the liability stream of a pension plan may be relatively small for a long time (i.e., a relatively young workforce), and it might be more appropriate to analyze risk based on longer time horizons. Goetzmann and Edwards (1994) have recently pointed out the problems of using the traditional one-year risk/return statistics for long-term planning, and the change to the traditional efficient frontier when longer-term statistics are incorporated into an analysis instead of the traditional one-year statistics. It should be emphasized again that pension plans can perform similar analyses incorporating a definition of risk that is the percent of the holding period returns below some benchmark or funding shortfall constraint.

Figure 9.3, taken from Bernstein, Pradhuman, and Barth (1993b), examines the risk/return characteristics of the S&P 500, and the previously defined growth, value, international stock, and small stock benchmarks. They define risk as the percent of the holding period returns that were negative; here that means the percent of the rolling five-year returns ending from 1975 to September 1993 during which the five-year total return was less than zero. The results are striking for several reasons. First, note that all the equity asset classes had higher absolute returns than did the S&P 500, again questioning the worth of long-term pension fund indexing to the S&P 500. In addition, value, international, and small stocks all lie northwest of the S&P 500, which suggests superior

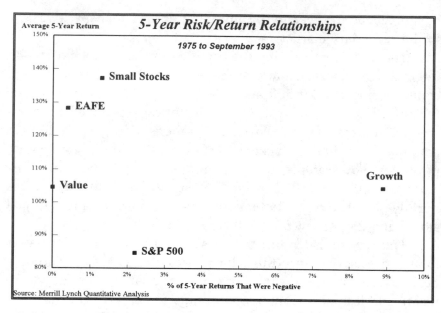

Figure 9.3 Risk/Return Combinations (Five-Year Holding Periods)

risk-adjusted returns as well. Second, note that value never had a negative five-year return during any of the rolling five-year holding periods within the eighteen-year period studied. Third, note that if one had to chose between growth and value, value would have probably been the better choice. Growth does offer slightly higher returns, but also had negative returns about 9 percent of the time, while value never had a five-year return that was negative.

Finally, they examined ten-year holding period returns, and one will immediately note that the probability of a negative return decreases substantially as one extends the time horizon used in the analysis. The result is that none of the equity asset groups ever had a negative ten-year return during the periods studied (ending 1980 to September 1990), meaning that asset allocation may be purely a function of return for true long-term time horizons. Thus, for truly long-term investors, or pension plans with truly long-term liabilities, investing in smaller capitalization stocks and international stocks makes the most sense because they have historically offered the highest returns.

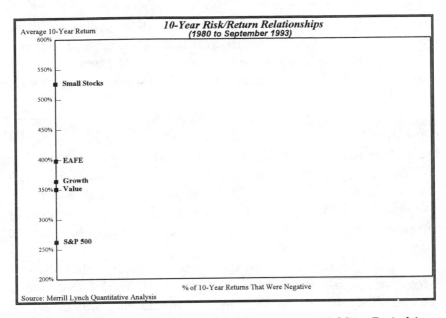

Figure 9.4   Risk/Return Combinations (Ten-Year Holding Periods)

Plan sponsors should also consider the duration of the equity portfolio, and whether the duration strategy of the equity portfolio is consistent with that of the fixed-income portfolio and with the goals of the overall pension plan. It is common to find the duration strategies of the equity and fixed-income portfolio moving in opposite directions, as the fixed-income manager prepares for a change in interest rates, while the equity managers are chasing the past performance of a strategy whose prior outperformance was fueled by the prior rise or fall in interest rates, which the fixed-income managers feel will soon end.

The duration of the equity portfolio should also be considered with respect to the liability stream, and whether the equity portion of the plan is contributing optimally toward the plan's anticipated cash flow outlays. Fixed-income portfolios, because of the lack of interaction between the discount rate and bond coupon payments, can be matched to plan liabilities, and those matches can be immunized against interest rate movements. In other words, bond portfolios can easily be constructed so that the durations of the bonds match the duration of the liabilities, and portfolios can be constructed with durations and convexities that will allow those matches to occur regardless of interest rate movements. Equity duration, however, is less precise because of the interaction between a stock's cash flow and the discount rate. Thus, one could not exact match with a portfolio of equities.

Equity portfolios can be constructed to augment a fixed-income duration matching strategy. There may be a case in which the plan is terribly underfunded, and fixed-income returns alone will not be high enough to match long-term funding needs. A potential strategy in that situation might be to exact match the liabilities for the short-term, and allow the longer-term returns of the equity market to grow the base capital of the plan to meet the longer-term funding needs.

It is fortunate that equities tend to outperform when interest rates fall because anticipated funding needs rise by definition when interest rates fall. The present value of the liability stream, which is used to determine present funding, will increase as the interest rate used to discount those future liabilities decreases. Thus, a firm could quickly become underfunded if their auditors believe that the discount rate that the firm is using to formulate the present value of the liabilities is too high, and they are forced to lower their discount rate. It is interesting to note that many corporations were still using discount rates in excess of 8 percent to 9 percent during 1993 despite that the thirty-year treasury bond yields fell below 6 percent in order to keep their anticipated liabilities lower and their funding status more healthy. A pure high-quality fixed-income portfolio might not have provided adequate returns to offset the potential funding shortfall that might have occurred simply because of a change in the discount rate.

◆ *Summary*

- ◆ As the equity market goes through phases during which styles of investing go in and out of favor, plan sponsors may want to strategically or tactically reallocate funds among managers, or "tilt" their overall plan toward a particular equity style.

♦ Style tilting strategies may be preferable to the traditional firing/hiring process because that process is costly and is usually based on hindsight.

♦ Pension assets should be diversified relative to the overall corporate assets to ensure survival of the pension plan should the company fail and to help prevent underfunding. Similarly, public pension funds should be careful regarding investments in local projects.

♦ Plan sponsors should determine if a manager is indeed a "good" manager by comparing the manager's performance to that of a representative peer group. When a style outperforms the overall market, even "bad" money managers may outperform traditional market benchmarks like the S&P 500. However, peer group evaluation must be done carefully because of managers' differing investment charters.

♦ Most corporate or strategic planning departments within a corporation provide much of the necessary forecasts needed for attempting to forecast active style rotation. The same forecasts that are used for running the corporation can be used to run the pension plan.

♦ Growth at a reasonable price (GARP) has become a popular equity management style, as equity managers attempt to smooth the cycles of growth and value investing. P/E-to-growth is one traditional GARP-type strategy.

♦ Plan sponsors must be aware of the risk imbedded into an equity portfolio. Unanticipated volatility can result in funding shortfalls.

♦ Plan sponsors should use several measures of portfolio risk in assessing equity strategy. The percent of the returns that fall below some required benchmark was suggested as a potentially insightful measure of risk.

♦ Time horizons can also be helpful in assessing the risk of an equity strategy.

♦ Plan sponsors should be sure to coordinate the duration-based strategies of the fixed-income and equity portfolios. It is not uncommon to see the duration of the fixed-income portfolio moving in one direction, while the duration of the equity portfolio is being adjusted in the opposite direction.

◆ References

Bailey, Jeffrey V. "Are Manager Universes Acceptable Performance Benchmarks?" *Journal of Portfolio Management*, Spring 1992, pp. 9–13.

Bernstein, Richard. "Thematic Tilting of Funds Among Equity Managers." *Merrill Lynch Pension Executive Review*, October 1990, pp. 7–12.

Bernstein, Richard, Pradhuman, Satya D., and Barth, Markus E. "Equity Asset Allocation—Part I: Risk, Return & Diversification." *Merrill Lynch Quantitative Viewpoint*, October 19, 1993.

Bernstein, Richard, Pradhuman, Satya D., and Barth, Markus E. "Equity Asset Allocation—Part II: Time Horizons." *Merrill Lynch Quantitative Viewpoint*, November 2, 1993.

Durand, David. "What Price Growth?" *Journal of Portfolio Management*, Fall 1992, pp. 84–91.

Franks, Edward Carr. "Targeting Excess-of-Benchmark Returns." *Journal of Portfolio Management*, Summer 1992, pp. 6–12.

Goetzmann, William N., and Edwards, Franklin R. "Short-Horizon Inputs and Long-Horizon Portfolio Choice." *Journal of Portfolio Management*, Summer 1994, pp. 76–81.

Harlow, W.V. "Asset Allocation in a Downside-Risk Framework." *Financial Analysts Journal*, September/October 1991, pp. 28–40.

Leibowitz, Martin L., Kogelman, Stanley, and Bader, Lawrence N. "Asset Performance and Surplus Control: A Dual-Shortfall Approach." *Journal of Portfolio Management*, Winter 1992, pp. 28–37.

Nigel, Adam. "Asset Allocation: Why Not Both?" *Plan Sponsor*, May 1994, pp. 42–43.

Peters, Donald. "Valuing a Growth Stock." *Journal of Portfolio Management*, Spring 1991, pp. 49–51.

Peters, Donald. *A Contrarian Strategy for Growth Stock Investing* (Westport, CT: Quorum Books), 1993.

10

Equity Derivatives and Style Investing

Derivatives are becoming increasingly popular among equity portfolio managers as the risk/return benefits of derivative instruments become better understood. However, some equity managers seem to be using derivative instruments without relation to their style of management, and simply look for buy and sell opportunities among derivatives, similar to the way they pick individual stocks. Picking derivatives like stocks may be an incorrect approach, and using the Earnings Expectations Life Cycle analogy, value-oriented managers should focus on buy-oriented derivative strategies, while growth-oriented managers should concentrate on sell-oriented derivative strategies.

The Earnings Expectations Life Cycle suggests that it is the buy decision that differentiates the "good" value manager from the "bad" value manager, but that it is the sell decision that separates the "good" growth manager from the "bad" growth manager. Thus, equity managers may want to pay attention to their investment styles when considering the use of derivative products. In particular, they should focus their use of derivatives around important performance turning-points that might ultimately differentiate them from their peer groups. This chapter first reviews the basic tenets of derivatives, in general, and specifically of put and call options. It then relates those concepts to style investing.

◆ What Is a Derivative?

As the name implies, derivatives are instruments that are derived from an existing tradable security or commodity. Rather than investing in an underlying asset (a company's stock, a T-Bond, or a pork belly), the investor can purchase a contract that provides the opportunity to trade in that underlying asset at some point in the future. Some derivative instruments trade on established exchanges such as the Chicago Board of Trade or the American Stock Exchange, while others are contracted between specific parties and are called over-the-counter (OTC) derivatives.

This chapter primarily focuses on equity derivatives, and there are many types of equity derivative instruments. Simpler derivatives are more widely used, while more complicated versions are generally used by a relatively small proportion of derivative users. The simplest derivative might be put or call options that entitle the option holder to the right, but not the obligation, to sell or buy a specified amount of an asset by a specified time. A standard call option might be the option to buy 100 shares of a stock at $50 per share by September 30, while a put option would be the option to sell 100 shares.

Equity Participation Notes (EPNs) are zero coupon, note-like instruments in terms of return of principal. However, the total return at maturity is determined by the performance of a specific equity index or basket of stocks. An example of an EPN might be a five-year zero coupon note whose eventual total return is determined by the performance of the S&P 500 during that five-year period. If the S&P 500 went down over the five-year period, then the worst return an investor would receive would be 0 percent, meaning the principal would be returned without interest. If the S&P 500 went up over the period, then the investor would receive some multiple of the S&P 500 appreciation as the "interest" on the original investment. Essentially, EPNs are bonds with a call option. In addition, EPNs can be structured differently for tax purposes

Another common derivative is called a *swap*. When they enter a swap agreement, the parties involved literally agree to swap or trade asset returns over a specified time period. For example, a stock investor might be wary of the stock market, while an insurance company might believe that its asset allocation is too heavily weighted toward cash. Rather than incurring the transaction costs of trading individual securities, those two parties might enter a swap agreement in which the stock investor paid the insurance company the quarterly return on the S&P 500, while the insurance company paid the stock investor the return of the 3-month T-Bill. Banks, insurance companies, and bond managers have used interest rate swaps for many years to help manage their funding costs and/or interest rate risk.

Derivatives can become more complicated by mixing calls and puts, mixing the specified times for delivery and underlying amounts within the contracts, and even mixing the underlying assets. In addition, derivative contracts can include their own imbedded options that might give the holder an opportunity to reset the terms of the contract at some future date, or release the holder from obligations if certain performance-related events occur. Those more complicated derivatives often carry the term *exotic*.

Leverage is very important within any discussion of derivatives. Because derivatives are based on the potential to buy or sell an asset, rather than on the actual underlying asset, one can invest a relatively small proportion of funds to get exposure equal to the full exposure of the underlying asset. For example, assume an investor had a choice between buying 100 shares of a stock at $70/share (a $7,000 investment) or purchasing call options to buy 100 shares of the stock at $60/share. The investor could buy seven contracts with the same $7,000 investment ($70−$60 × 100 shares = $1,000/contract). Now assume that the stock price rises to $80. The investor who bought the stock itself would have a 14.3 percent return (the percent change from $70 to $80). Option investors would have doubled their money because the option contracts would have risen from $10/contract to $20/contract, and the overall option investment would be worth $14,000 ($80−$60 × 100 shares = $2,000/contract. Seven contracts at $2,000/contract equals $14,000). Of course, the leverage would work against the option holder if the stock price had fallen to $60. In that case, the option portfolio would have lost nearly its entire value versus only a 14.3 percent loss for the stock investor.

◆ The Risks of Equity Derivatives

There are several risks associated with equity derivative instruments beyond the volatility risk that is often associated with them. There is also credit risk, procedural and "oversight" risk, and the risk that the derivatives market itself does not function properly (liquidity risk). While most derivative market participants go to great lengths to limit the risks associated with derivatives, it is obviously impossible for each participant to fully guard against all potential risks.

Volatility risk is that risk associated with the overall volatility of the financial markets. In other words, derivatives are priced, and expectations are set, based on historical and implied volatility relationships. Some have questioned whether a significant change in overall market volatility might cause a market "meltdown" because derivative issuers have not anticipated extreme changes in volatility. Although volatility risk does indeed exist, it probably could not, in and of itself, cause a market "meltdown." Most derivative issuers go to great extremes to hedge themselves against potential increases or decreases in overall market volatility. An individual issuer's profitability might be reduced significantly from poorly established hedges, but the probability of a full "meltdown" is most likely to be quite low.

Credit risk is also a potential source of risk. Similar to bonds, derivatives are financial contracts. A counterparty's ability to make good on a particular contract is obviously essential to the process. The probability of credit risk may rise during recessions, when overall corporate and financial cash flows tend to be strained.

Some have raised the issue that the equity derivatives market is too illiquid to function properly under periods of market duress. One should always be concerned about a market's liquidity regardless of whether that market is derivatives- or cash-based. Most OTC derivatives can be broken down into components (i.e., a stock and an exchange listed option, and so on), and there is often significant amounts of liquidity in the listed markets associated with those component parts. Thus, even if the OTC market became terribly illiquid, the liquid-listed markets might provide adequate liquidity to allow one to offset an existing derivative position.

The least often discussed, but perhaps a large source of risk, is what is called procedural or "control" risk. That is the risk that occurs because derivative market participants do not have adequate oversight or monitoring procedures in place. Such monitoring would include legal, audit, and risk management procedures. Some now-famous corporate losses supposedly caused by derivatives may have been more a result of procedural risk than of anything else.

◆ *A Brief History of Derivatives*

Contrary to what one might believe reading the popular press, derivative instruments are certainly not new. According to Hieronymus (1977), commodity and agricultural futures and forward contracts date back to medieval fairs in the 1200s, and the first options, which were tied to pig iron, were supposedly to have begun trading during the early 1700s in England. The initiation of modern exchange futures trading, as we now know it, dovetailed with the founding of the Chicago Board of Trade in 1848.

Financial-related, as opposed to commodity-related, derivatives have also traded for some time, but gained in credibility with the opening of exchanges for financial futures and options. The Chicago Board of Options Exchange opened in 1973, and served to add breadth and depth to the stock options market. The first interest rate–related futures began trading in October 1975, when the Chicago Board of Trade began to trade GNMA futures. That was followed in January 1976 by the Chicago Mercantile Exchange's 3-month T-Bill future.

The OTC derivatives market has grown in size substantially over the past five to ten years, with interest rate– and currency–related derivatives comprising the largest portion of that market.

Recently, one of the fastest growth segments of the OTC derivative market has centered on equities and equity indices. Equity investors have discovered that OTC derivatives sometimes allow greater flexibility than do exchange listed derivatives. In addition, the spread of global investing has led investors to use the OTC derivatives market as a means for gaining cost-effective international exposure.

◆ The Basics of Put and Call Options

Buyers of stock-related options have the option, but not the obligation, to buy or sell some specified amount of a stock, a portfolio of stocks, or an established index within a specified period of time. Call options are options to buy stock; put options are options to sell. Some options allow the holder to exercise the option at any point during the specified time period (American options), while others permit the option to be exercised only at expiration (European options).

An interesting feature of options is that, in most cases, the maximum loss that the option holder can incur is the cost of the option itself. For example, if one bought an option to buy stock at $10 per share, but the actual price of the stock was only $5 per share at option expiration, then the option would expire worthless. After all, who would pay $10 per share under the option contract when he or she can pay $5 per share in the open market? Thus, the maximum investment loss, in dollar terms, is generally known.

This is not a treatise on the mathematics of option valuation, but it may be worthwhile to review a few simple concepts. Cox and Rubinstein (1985), in perhaps the bible of sophisticated options theory, point out that the value of an option can be influenced by a number of factors. We will review only the major factors here:

1. *The current stock price*   The higher the stock price, generally the higher the call option value and the lower the put value.

2. *The strike price of the option*   The higher the strike price, generally the lower the call option value and the higher the put value.

3. *Time to expiration* The longer the time to expiration of the option, generally the higher both the put and call option value because the probability that the underlying stock or stocks will do extremely well or extremely poorly is higher over the long term.

4. *Stock volatility* The higher the volatility of the underlying stock or stocks, generally the higher both the put and call option value because the probability rises that the stock will do either very well or very poorly.

5. *Interest rates* As interest rates rise, the present value of the strike price declines, and we return to #2 in the list. As interest rates rise, the present value of the strike price declines and the value of the call goes up, while the value of the put declines.

6. *Cash dividends* The holder of the option does not receive the dividends of the underlying stock. Thus, the larger the proportion of total return that is made up of dividends, generally the lower the call option value. Note that the price of over-the-counter, tailored options may be adjusted for the dividend stream depending on the particular option.

There are other significant factors that can affect option values. Some may be the expected growth rate of the underlying stock, the relative value of the underlying stock compared to other assets, investor risk preferences, taxes and transaction costs.

Figure 10.1 shows the potential advantages to options. The analysis assumes that one would have purchased a one-year call option on the S&P 500 index, and then compares the distribution of the actual S&P 500 one-year total returns from 1926 to 1992 with the price returns of the hypothetical call option. Price returns are used for the call option because the holder would not receive any dividend payments over the one-year life of the option. The analysis did not include any transaction costs either for the S&P 500 or for the hypothetical option. The graph's horizontal axis shows twelve-month potential returns ranging from −30 percent or less to +30 percent or more, broken into 5 percent increments.

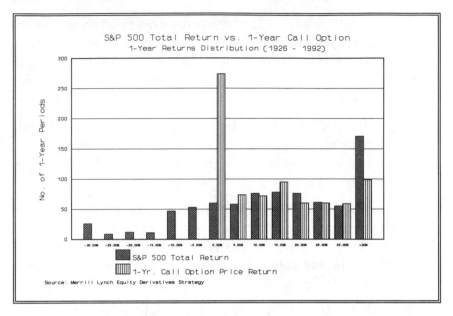

Figure 10.1 Returns Distribution: S&P 500 Total Return vs. One-Year Call Options

The vertical axis measures the number of times that twelve-month returns fell within one of the return buckets. It is important to understand that the returns for the call option and the S&P 500 for a specific period may not fall into the same return slot. For example, suppose the S&P 500 total return was 17 percent for a given twelve-month period, while that for the option was 14 percent.

The returns distribution of the hypothetical call option is constrained relative to that of the actual S&P 500. The upper portion is constrained because the option holder does not receive dividends. That may seem trivial within the context of the current equity market in which dividend yields are less than 3 percent; however, the lack of dividends does have the potential to make a sizable difference between price return and total return, especially at market troughs when dividend yields are often at their highest. Note that S&P 500 total returns were greater than 30 percent during more than 150 of the twelve-month periods, while the price return of the call option was greater than 30 percent fewer than 100 times.

More important, note that the lower end of the distribution of option returns is completely constrained so that there are no negative returns. As already stated, the maximum loss of an option is generally the cost of the option itself and, thus, the minimum return within the example would be 0 because we are not including transaction costs in the analysis.

◆ Hedging

In any derivatives market, whether it be financial or commodity, there are generally three types of participants: investors, speculators, and hedgers. Investors use derivatives to take risk-controlled active positions, and search for situations in which investing using a derivative provides a superior risk/return profile than investing in the underlying security itself. For example, purchasing an EPN tied to the MSCI-EAFE index might provide some investors with superior risk/return potential relative to an index fund that mimicked the index, and might also help to alleviate the custody, transaction cost, and currency problems that can be associated with international investing (see Bernstein, 1994b).

Speculators seek additional risk in order to get superior returns. They make a "bet" on the direction of the underlying asset, and then utilize the leverage imbedded in a derivative instrument to turn a small cash outlay into a significant position. Hedge funds, despite their name, generally use derivatives for speculative purposes. The modern hedge fund takes a stand on a stock, stock market, currency, or bond market, and then uses the leverage of derivatives to significantly accentuate its potential.

Hedgers use derivatives to control the risk of an existing underlying investment. For example, an equity portfolio manager, who might be required to be fully invested and therefore cannot raise cash, might want to protect a portfolio against a market correction by buying S&P 500 put options.

Hedges are combinations of options with the underlying stock portfolio of stocks or index so that the range of potential return outcomes is better known than by investing in the underlying alone. If one were to invest in the underlying stock, portfolio of stocks, or index alone (sometimes called a naked or uncovered position), then the range of potential return outcomes is relatively unknown. Of course, one probably thought one had some insight regarding potential outcomes, otherwise one probably would not have invested at all, but hedging may still remove some, or all, of the remaining uncertainty.

Figure 10.2 illustrates the concept of constraining the range of possible investment outcomes by hedging. In the example, we compare the one-year total returns of the S&P 500 with the one-year returns of a portfolio of 90 percent S&P 500 and 10 percent S&P 50-put options. (To simplify the example, we assume that at-the-money puts were always available.) The reruns of the hedged combination are constrained at the tails of the distribution, and the S&P 500 alone had more periods in which returns were greater than 35 percent and more periods during which the returns were less than −10 percent. The cost of hedging is that the extremely

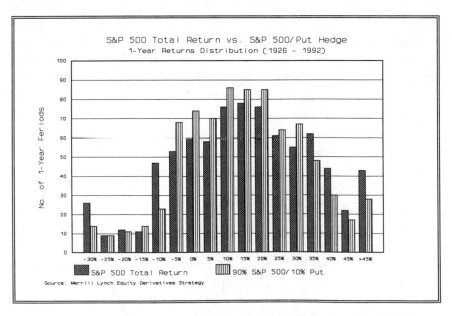

Figure 10.2   Returns Distribution: Hedged vs. Unhedged S&P 500 Port-folios

good periods tend to be given up; the effectiveness of the hedge is that there are fewer extremely bad periods.

The combination of S&P 500 and S&P 500 put options is not really a good long-term strategy because the S&P 500 trends upward through time. Thus, it might be better long-term strategy to simply buy and hold the S&P 500. However, institutional investors do not necessarily have the luxury of true long-term time horizons, nor does the *relative* performance of all styles trend upward over the long term. For example, it was demonstrated that if one invested in smaller capitalization stocks at the wrong time, it might take many years before one would be satisfied with one's investment. In fact, using the Earnings Expectations Life Cycle, the potential need for hedging increases as the consensus becomes more certain regarding the potential positive or negative outcome of an investment.

◆ Reviewing the Earnings Expectations Life Cycle

To review, growth-oriented managers tend to pick stocks in the upper half of the Life Cycle because they tend to be high-expectations managers. Value managers, on the other hand, tend to pick stocks in the bottom portion because they tend to be low-expectations managers. "Good" managers, regardless of style, tend to be on the left side of the Life Cycle because they will tend to buy stocks with rising expectations. "Bad" managers, however, will tend to fall on the right side of the Life Cycle because they will tend to buy or hold stocks with falling expectations. Overlaying Figures 10.3 to 10.6 on top of each other demonstrates where on the cycle the "good" growth manager, the "bad" growth manager, the "good" value manager, and the "bad" value manager would lie. Figure 10.7 shows the "good" versus "bad" combined with growth versus value.

For growth managers, note that the "good" growth manager sits between 9 o'clock and midnight, while the "bad" growth manager sits between midnight and 3 o'clock. This implies that what differentiates the "good" from the "bad" growth manager is not

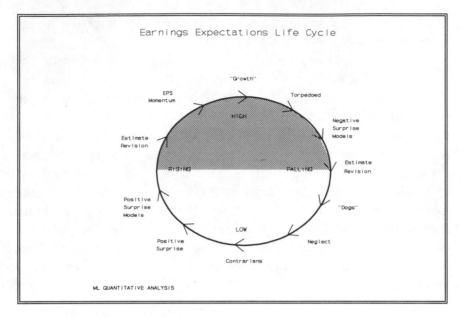

Figure 10.3 Growth Managers

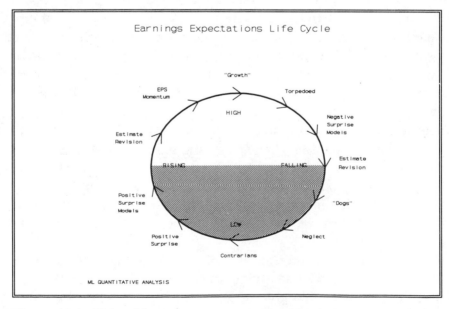

Figure 10.4 Value Managers

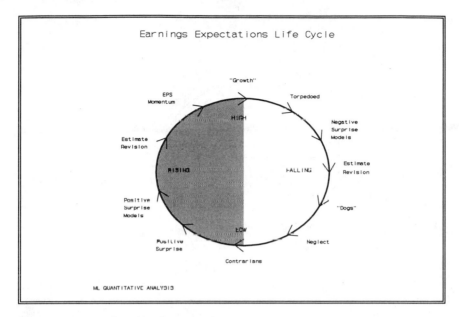

Figure 10.5 "Good" Managers

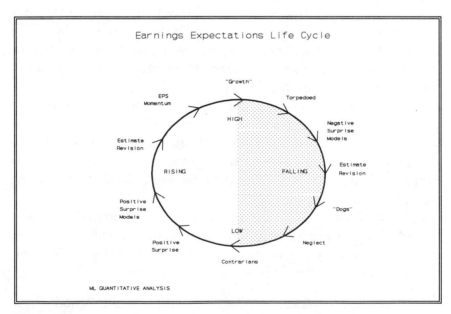

Figure 10.6 "Bad" Managers

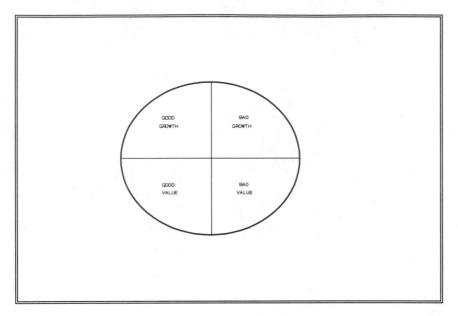

Figure 10.7   "Good" vs. "Bad" Combined with Growth vs. Value

necessarily which stocks one is buying, but rather, which stocks one is selling. Contrarians are often thought of as value managers who buy out-of-favor stocks, but the Earnings Expectations Life Cycle suggests that successful growth managers must be contrarians as well, except that they must *sell* stocks that the consensus views extremely favorably.

For the value manager, the "good" value manager sits between 6 o'clock and 9 o'clock, while the "bad" value manager sits between 3 o'clock and 6 o'clock. This appears to confirm the traditional idea of a contrarian, and suggests that value manager performance is more likely to be hurt by buying early than by holding too long.

If the theory behind the Earnings Expectations Life Cycle is correct, and the key to successful style management depends on the manager's willingness to be a contrarian, then the implications regarding derivative strategies may be as follows:

◆ Because contrarian selling may differentiate "good" from "bad" growth managers, growth managers may want to utilize derivatives to make the returns distributions around *selling* points more certain.

♦ Because contrarian buying may differentiate "good" from "bad" value managers, value managers may want to utilize derivatives to make the returns distributions around *buying* points more certain.

Two case studies will attempt to support these contentions. The first involves value managers and the potential purchase of bank stocks during 1990, while the second involves growth managers and the potential sale of drug stocks during 1992.

Case Study 1: Value Managers and Bank Stocks During 1990

In early 1990, bank stocks began to appear on some value managers' buy lists. The industry group had experienced sizable secular pressures that had left several of America's largest banks selling at price-to-book value ratios substantially less than 1.0. Some value managers began to buy bank stocks in early 1990 because of what appeared to be compelling valuations.

Unfortunately, the stocks underperformed dramatically until November 1990 as the market began to discount the cyclical pressures that the bank group was experiencing because of the recession. What were perceived to be undervalued situations merely became more and more undervalued as the year progressed. Value managers who held substantial proportions of their portfolios in the banking sector significantly underperformed the market and underperformed other value managers who did not have such large exposures to banks.

A more risk adverse strategy might have been to buy a call option on the banking industry or a selected portfolio of bank stocks rather than investing in the bank stocks outright. A call option would have allowed the holder to *synthetically overweight* the group. The leverage incorporated into an option (that is, not having to actually buy 100 shares to fully participate in the price movement of 100 shares) would have allowed value managers to commit a smaller portion of their funds to the bank group, yet would have allowed managers to fully participate in any upside performance that the group might have experienced. If the group under-performed, as they did, then managers would have been able to gauge their worst case scenarios because the maximum loss of an option is generally the cost of the option itself. Instead of investing in stocks that lost 50 percent of their value, option holders might have potentially lost less than even 10 percent. (The cost of the option is here assumed to be 10 percent or less. The actual cost of the option would have been determined by characteristics similar to those presented in the first part of this chapter.)

Case Study 2: Growth Managers and Drug Stocks in 1992

The S&P Drug Index rose 61 percent during 1991, and that performance contributed greatly to some growth managers superior performance during that year. However, despite data that showed that earnings expectations for the industry had actually peaked as 1991 progressed and began to decline at the turn of the year, growth-oriented investors generally continued to consider the drug stocks to be among the most attractive groups in the market. During 1992, that decision to continue overweighting the drug group led some growth managers to significantly underperform the overall market as the Drug Index fell nearly 22 percent.

Keeping in mind that it is the sell decision that may separate "good" from "bad" growth stock managers, it might have made more sense to *synthetically underweight* the drug industry using derivatives than to simply hold the stocks alone. The leverage in-corporated into an option (not having to actually sell 100 shares to fully protect against the price decline of 100 shares) would have allowed growth managers to protect a larger portion of their total funds invested in the drug group, yet would have allowed them to participate in any upside performance that the group might have experienced. If the group had outperformed, which it did not, then managers would have been able to gauge their cost of protection because the maximum loss of an option is generally the cost of the option itself. Thus, growth managers who held a drug put option might have suffered considerably less than did their peers who held the stocks alone. The impact to the total portfolio might have been as though the managers had underweighted the drug group.

◆ *Potential for Improving Peer Group Relative Performance*

Institutional money management has increasingly become a relative performance derby. Whereas plan sponsors used to be concerned about absolute performance, today's more sophisticated performance measurement techniques and creative index funds now tend to force managers to concern themselves with performance relative to their stated benchmark or to their peer group. The relative performance race appears to have somewhat changed the goal from consistently increasing capital wealth to being a top quintile manager.

Incorporating derivatives into the active investment process to synthetically overweight and underweight industries or sectors may potentially improve relative performance. Figure 10.8 compares one-year relative performance versus the S&P 500 of a portfolio that included an investment made in the S&P Money Center Bank group versus one that included an investment in a one-year Money Center Bank call option (synthetically overweighting). We assume the first portfolio contains a 5 percent weight in the Money Center Group (roughly three times the 1.6% that it represented within the S&P 500 at the beginning of the period) and a 95 percent investment in the remainder of the S&P 500. The second portfolio contains a 0.5 percent weight in a one-year call option on the Money Center Banks and a 99.5 percent investment in the remainder of the S&P 500. That 0.5 percent weight again assumes that the option would cost about 10 percent of the original notional amount (0.10 times 5 percent). The option could be a smaller proportion of the total portfolio, but would offer similar exposure to the 5 percent weight in the original portfolio because of the option's imbedded leverage. The 5 percent versus 0.5 percent demonstrates

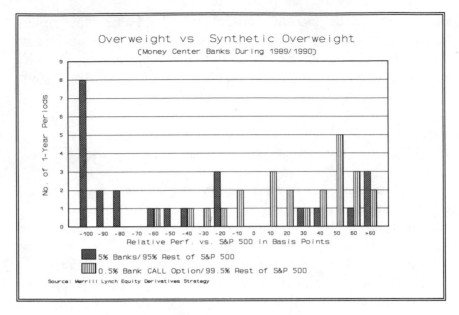

Figure 10.8   Overweight vs. Synthetic Overweight

the potential significant difference in portfolio weighting schemes that a synthetic overweight strategy might achieve.

The figure suggests that the manager who actually invested in the Money Center Bank group during the period could have underperformed the S&P 500 by more than 100 basis points simply because of the 5 percent weight in the bank group. In fact, the manager would have underperformed the S&P 500 by at least 80 basis points during twelve of the twenty-four months studied, solely because of the bank overweight. Compare that to the 60 basis point worst underperformance (which only occurred once, by the way) of the portfolio in which banks were synthetically over-weighted. Thus, during 1989 and 1990, when value managers were generally suffering from their exposures to financial stocks, the value manager who synthetically overweighted the Money Center Banks instead of actually overweighting them might have had at least a 40 basis point relative performance advantage over the over value managers. In fact, the portfolio with the synthetic overweight outperformed the S&P 500 during 75 percent of the one-year periods studied, while the portfolio with the actual overweight underperformed during 75 percent of the periods.

Figure 10.9 compares the strategies discussed in the second case study, and examines the returns distribution of a portfolio with 15 percent exposure to the S&P Drugs (again, roughly three times its weight in the index) with a portfolio that incorporates the synthetic underweighting of the group. Again, the synthetic underweight strategy buys a put option on the industry so that the net exposure, when taking account of the option's leverage, would be similar to underweighting the group. In the example in the figure, the synthetic underweight is built from the original 15 percent drug exposure, and is comprised of a 1.5 percent investment in a one-year S&P Drugs put option and a 13.5 percent exposure in the S&P drugs.

Figure 10.9, like Figure 10.8, examines performance relative to the S&P 500, and the synthetic underweight constrains the returns distribution so that the number of periods during which the actual overweight portfolio underperformed the S&P 500 by at least 200 basis points purely because of the drug exposure was cut from

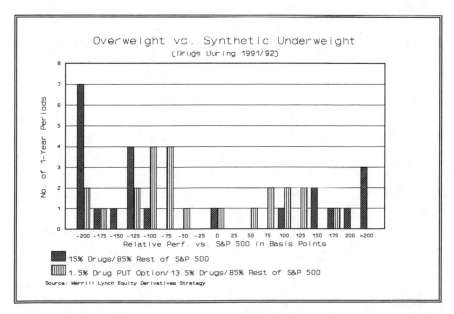

Figure 10.9 Overweight vs. Synthetic Underweight

seven to two. During the worst one-year period, the true over-weighted portfolio underperformed the S&P 500 by 417 basis points, while the synthetic underweight portfolio underperformed by 226 basis points. Thus, the synthetic underweight, which attempts to hedge an existing exposure, contributed nearly 200 basis points of relative performance versus the S&P 500. Growth managers who had undertaken such a strategy during this period would have probably significantly outperformed other growth managers who maintained sizable uncovered drug exposures.

◆ Overlay Strategies for Plan Sponsors

Asset reallocation strategies have changed significantly during the past ten years. Whereas plan sponsors used to reallocate strategies by shifting funds from bond managers to equity managers, and vice versa, or by hiring balanced managers who would themselves shift funds from stocks to bonds to cash, plan sponsors today increasingly hire managers who remain fully invested in a particular asset class and use derivatives to "overlay" an asset allocation on top of the fund managers. For example, if the fund's assets are generally in bonds, but the sponsor believes that a tactical shift toward equities might be appropriate, then the plan sponsor, or a tactical allocation manager hired by the sponsor, might sell bond futures and buy S&P 500 futures, which would synthetically shift the assets. The main advantages to the overlay strategies is that they are immediate and relatively cheap. Shifting funds from one manager to another takes time, whereas buying and selling futures is instantaneous. Shifting funds can be costly because of the transaction costs involved in selling assets out of one fund and buying assets into the other. In addition, while funds are shifting, and until they are reinvested, they will reside in cash. That means that the goal might have been to shift from bonds to stocks, but the end result (at least for a period of time) was to shift from bonds to cash.

Plan sponsors should now consider the very real possibility of overlaying style rotation as well. Rather than shifting funds from growth managers to value managers, or from large capitalization managers to smaller capitalization managers, or from high-quality managers to low-quality managers, the plan sponsor can buy or sell a derivative that would help to gain or reduce the exposure of a particular style.

The cost of such derivatives, however, should be weighed against the cost of manager transition. Today's sophisticated program trading techniques greatly reduce the transaction costs of manager transitions and, thus, the cost of a derivative overlay should not be judged only in terms of risk/return or added return, but also in terms of its cost relative to alternative means of gaining or reducing exposure.

Plan sponsors who rely heavily on high-quality managers might want to continually overlay a strategy to remove the quality distinction from their plan, and rely on their high-quality managers purely for their stock selection expertise. That might sound strange because why would one want to synthetically lower the quality of the overall equity portion of the plan? As we tried to point out earlier, lower-quality stocks tend to outperform higher-quality stocks, and much of that performance strength comes from ratings drift. Ratings drift traditionally refers to changes in bond rating. Bond rating agencies tend to raise the ratings of the bonds whose fundamentals are improving, and tend to lower those of companies whose fundamentals are deteriorating. Studies on ratings drift have found that the ratings of the highest-quality companies tend to decrease through time, while those of the least healthy companies tend to improve through time. Thus, through time it might be preferable to have a marginally lower-quality portfolio, and equity derivatives allow the plan sponsor to synthetically lower the quality of the overall equity plan without the need for intensive individual stock research and bankruptcy assessment.

◆ Summary

- ◆ Derivatives are becoming increasingly popular among equity portfolio mangers, however, some equity managers use derivatives strategies without consideration for their equity style.

♦ Derivatives are contracts that provide the opportunity to trade in an asset at some specified point in the future.

♦ Leverage is very important within any discussion of derivatives. One can invest a relatively small proportion of funds to get exposure equal to the full exposure of the underlying asset.

♦ Derivatives do indeed have their risks. Those risks include volatility risk, credit risk, "oversight" risk, and liquidity risk.

♦ Options are derivatives contracts, but not obligations, to buy or sell a specific amount of stock or stocks at a specific price by a specific time.

♦ Some of the main factors that affect option pricing are the stock price, the strike price of the option, the time to expiration, the underlying stock volatility, interest rates, and dividends.

♦ Options tend to offer a more predictable returns distribution than do stocks.

♦ Hedges are combinations of options with the underlying stock, portfolio of stocks, or index so that the range of potential return outcomes is better known than by investing in the underlying alone.

♦ The need for hedging equity portfolios may increase as the consensus becomes more certain about the positive or negative outcome of a particular investment.

♦ One conclusion of the Life Cycle analogy is that contrarian buying separates "good" from "bad" value managers, but contrarian selling separates "good" from "bad" growth managers. The success of style investing may depend on a particular manager's willingness to be a contrarian.

◆ Because it is sometimes difficult to be a contrarian, value managers should focus on derivative strategies to make the returns distributions around buy points more certain. Growth managers should focus on strategies that make the returns distributions around sell points more certain.

◆ Derivatives allow the investor to be more of a contrarian because of the risk control that they offer.

◆ Given that institutional money management is increasingly becoming a relative performance derby, it may be increasingly beneficial for portfolio managers to begin to incorporate derivatives into traditional portfolio management.

◆ Plan sponsors are increasingly using derivatives to overlay style rotation strategies much the same way they now overlay asset allocation changes.

◆ The cost of such style rotation overlay strategies should be weighed against the cost of today's sophisticated program trading technology. The time it takes to complete a manager transition between equity managers has been reduced substantially.

◆ Additionally, derivatives can be used to synthetically lower the quality of the equity portfolio without the need for intensive individual stock research and bankruptcy assessment.

◆ References

Bernstein, Richard. "Equity Derivatives & Style Investing." *Merrill Lynch Equity Derivatives Strategy—Special Report*, June 1993.

Bernstein, Richard. "Derivatives: Why All The Attention?" *Merrill Lynch Equity Derivatives Strategy Update*, April 19, 1994.

Bernstein, Richard. "Derivatives and Country Rotation." *Merill Lynch Equity Derivatives Strategy Update*, April 26, 1994.

Bernstein, Richard. "A Guide to Exchange Listed Derivatives." *Merrill Lynch Equity Derivatives Stragegy-Special Report*, August 18, 1994.

Cox, John R. and Rubinstein, Mark. *Options Markets* (Englewood Cliffs, NJ: Prentice Hall), 1985.

Hieronymus, Thomas A. *Economics of Futures Trading, for Commercial and Personal Profit, 2nd Edition* (New York: Commodity Research Bureau), 1977.

11

Implications for the Disciplined and Long-Term Investor

*T*he bulk of the material in this book has focused on the performance cycles of market segments and their effects on style investing. The product bought and sold in the equity market is nominal profits growth, and expectations regarding the abundance or scarcity of that nominal profits growth set the stage for style performance. When investor expectations are optimistic, meaning that nominal profits growth is expected to become increasingly abundant, investors will generally bid up the prices of the stocks that comprise riskier market segments. When expectations become more pessimistic, then investors will shun the riskier segments of the equity market, and will invest in "safe haven" segments. It is the perception or, better yet, the misperception and not the reality of what is safe or risky that presents the opportunity for the contrarian.

Many market segments outlined in this book actually follow similar expectation-based rules of performance regardless of how one defines those segments. Smaller capitalization stocks will tend to outperform larger ones, lower-quality stocks will tend to outperform higher-quality ones, higher beta stocks will tend to outperform lower beta ones, value stocks will tend to outperform growth stocks, and so on, when expectations regarding future nominal growth grow increasingly optimistic. Those are the riskier market segments. Larger stocks, higher-quality stocks, lower beta stocks, growth stocks, and so forth are the safer market segments and will tend to outperform as pessimism builds.

Eventually, the consensus perceives that the riskier segments may not be so risky after all, they shun the safe segments because their profits growth is inferior, and because safe stocks are under-performing. That newly formed consensus slowly builds strength until it reaches complete unanimity, which probably occurs at a profits cycle peak. For instance, it was demonstrated that dividend growth rates are an excellent example of the consensus not wanting to act when times seem bad, but very willing to act at the peak, when everything seems fine. Corporations are loathe to raise div-idends soon after a recession for fear that the prematurely raised dividend will have to be cut, sending a signal to the marketplace that not only are the company's prospects poor, but management may not know what it is doing. However, dividend growth rates are usually quite high at the peak of an economic cycle. There are similar examples for safe segments as well. Everyone loves growth stocks at the trough of the economic cycle, just at a point at which one should be shunning growth and reorienting one's portfolio for economic sensitivity.

Some readers may feel that the topics discussed in this book do not apply to them for a couple of reasons. Number one, they might feel that they follow a disciplined style approach, and to switch styles according to the cycles in this book would force them from time to time to violate those disciplines. Number two, they may feel that they are long-term investors rather than market timers or sector rotators, and that this book has focused on shorter-term cycles. This chapter addresses those two issues. Following a specific discipline is probably a sound strategy, nevertheless, one should be prepared for significant periods of time during which the dis-cipline does not work. In addition, long-term investors should make sure that their long-term strategies do indeed outperform the mar-ket over the long term.

Bernstein and Pradhuman (1994) studied the long-term rel-ative performance trends of roughly thirty different stock-picking methodologies based on the relative performance of equal-weighted portfolios that were rebalanced monthly versus the equal-weighted S&P 500. They found that relative performance trends varied widely by stock-picking methodology, and that the relative performance trends were substantially different even among stock-picking methods that focused on the same style. They computed log linear trendlines according to the following simple regression:

$$Log(RELPERF) = a + b(TIME),$$

where,

RELPERF = the relative performance versus the equal-weighted S&P 500 of a particular stock-picking method,

TIME = a time series that increments by 1.0 each month.

The resulting trendlines measured the average increase in relative performance per month simply because of the passage of time. A better way of thinking of trendlines is that they represent the long-term relative performance one might have experienced if one had not attempted to time the cycles of growth and value investing, and simply maintained a single and consistent investment style. Figure 11.1 is an example of how the trendline relates to the actual relative performance using the returns of High Earnings Yield.

One might suppose that these trendlines would be very similar for characteristics that fall within the same style category. That did not appear to be true. Figure 11.2 shows the long-term performance trends for four value-oriented characteristics: Earnings Yield, Low Price/Book Value, Low Price/Cash Flow, and Low Price/Sales. The long-term relative performance trendlines for Earnings Yield and Low Price/Cash Flow slope upward suggesting that they generally outperformed the overall equity market over the nine-year period studied, while those for Low Price/Book and Low Price/Sales were downward sloping. Thus, the statement that value outperforms over the long-term may depend on one's definition of value.

Figure 11.3 shows the long-term relative performance trendlines for several growth-oriented characteristics. The trendlines of all three of the strategies shown, EPS Surprise, EPS Momentum,

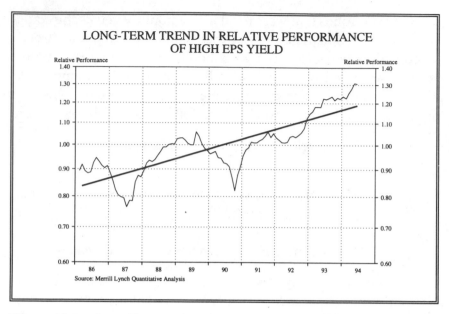

Figure 11.1 Long-Term Relative Performance Trendline of High Earnings Yield

and Projected Five-Year EPS Growth, do indeed slope upward, although the relative performance trend of EPS Surprise is substantially steeper than those of the other two. (In earlier chapters, EPS Estimate Revision was included as another growth-oriented stock-picking method. The Merrill Lynch database has data on EPS Estimate Revision beginning only in 1989. Estimate Revision was omitted from this section because it might be misleading to compare a trendline that was computed using data beginning in 1989 with those based on data that began in 1986.)

Figures 11.4 and 11.5 compare the long-term relative performance trendlines for high- and low-quality stocks. Figure 11.4 shows the cumulative relative performance of C- and D-rated stocks (according to Standard & Poor's Common Stock Ratings) and the long-term relative performance trendline. The distinctly upward sloping trendline suggests that investing in lower-quality stocks has been a very successful long-term strategy. Figure 11.5 shows the relative performance of A+-rated stocks. The relative performance trendline of A+ stocks is actually flat, which suggests

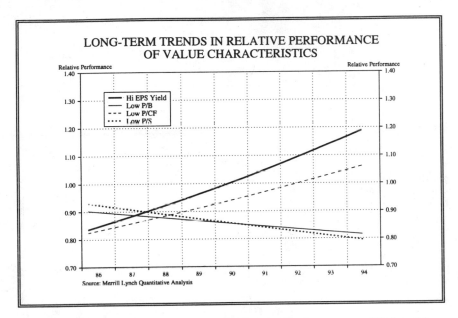

Figure 11.2 Long-Term Trends in Relative Performance of Value Characteristics

that they are merely performing in-line with the overall equity market over the long term, and that managers that focus on high-quality stocks must derive superior performance from stock selection rather than relying solely on the high quality strategy.

Figures 11.6 to 11.21 are the relative performance charts and long-term relative performance trendlines for a large group of stock selection methods. The two potential objections regarding disciplined approaches to investing and long-term investing should be answered in the examination of these figures. Disciplined investing is probably a sound approach to investment management (as opposed to somewhat random stock picking or "shooting from the hip"); however, one should be prepared for periods of significant relative underperformance even if the strategy performs well over the long term. There are long and severe periods of relative underperformance even in the cases of the best growth- and value-oriented strategies (High EPS Surprise and High Earnings Yield). Although earnings yield has one of the steepest long-term relative performance trendlines, it still significantly underperformed during

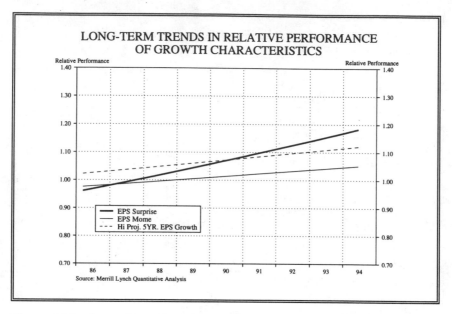

Figure 11.3 Long-Term Trends in Relative Performance of Growth Characteristics

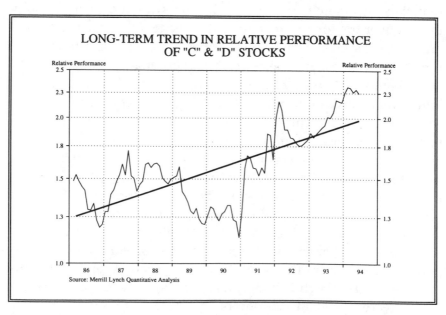

Figure 11.4 Long-Term Trend in Relative Performance of C and D Stocks

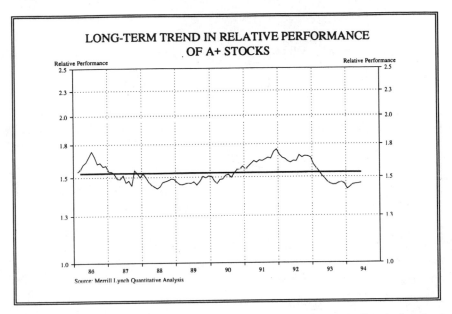

Figure 11.5 Long-Term Trend in Relative Performance of A+ Stocks

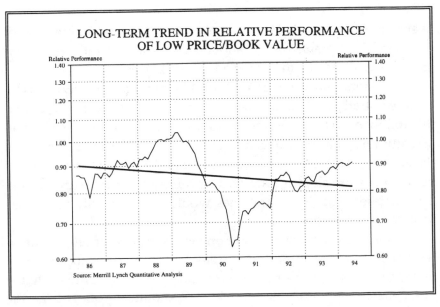

Figure 11.6 Long-Term Trend in Relative Performance of Low Price/ Book Value

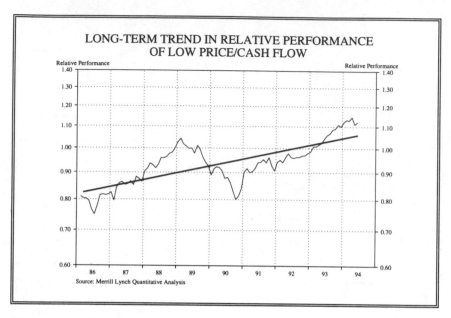

Figure 11.7 Long-Term Trend in Relative Performance of Low Price/ Cash Flow

nearly all of 1989 and 1990. Surely some traditional Low P/E or Earnings Yield managers questioned the worth of following their disciplined strategies toward the end of that period.

Investors must be careful in selecting a long-term style-oriented strategy, because many of the style-related strategies on the following pages only seem to work on a cyclical basis, and actually underperform over the long term. For example, most of the quality categories that were discussed in Chapter 5 actually have downward sloping long-term relative performance trendlines. That implies that those strategies would have actually underperformed over the long term.

Thus, regardless of whether one is disciplined or one is a long-term investor, it is important to pay close attention to style and market segment performance. One can probably surmise that if everyone is suggesting that stock XYZ should be bought for the long term, it is probably not a good idea to do so. Similarly, if everyone reads this book and decides that Earnings Yield is the

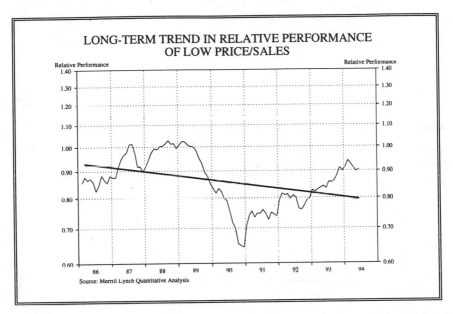

Figure 11.8 Long-Term Trend in Relative Performance of Low Price/ Sales

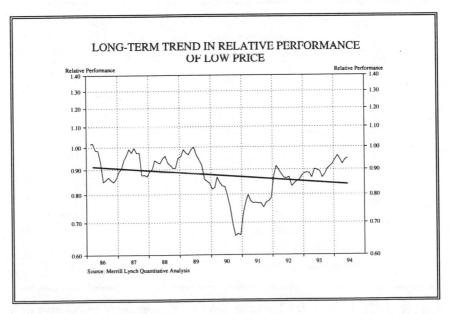

Figure 11.9 Long-Term Trend in Relative Performance of Low Price

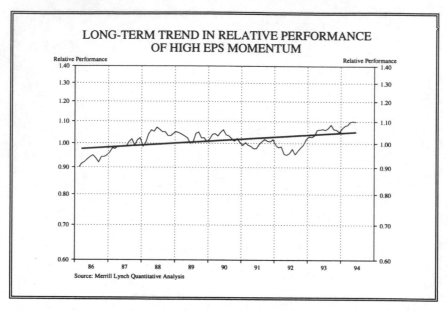

Figure 11.10   Long-Term Trend in Relative Performance of High EPS Momentum

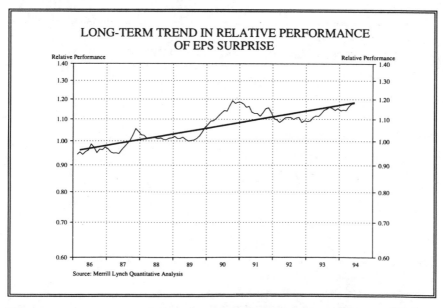

Figure 11.11   Long-Term Trend in Relative Performance of Positive EPS Surprise

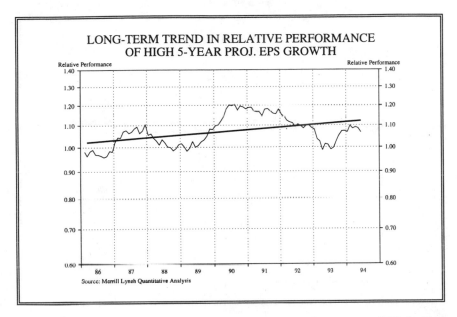

Figure 11.12 Long-Term Trend in Relative Performance of High Projected Five-Year Earnings Growth

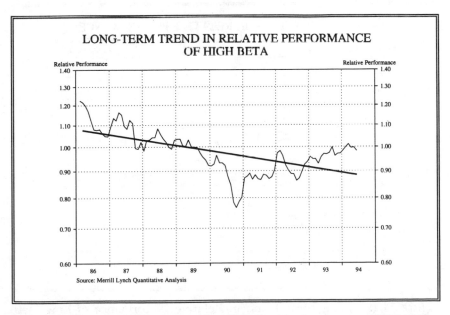

Figure 11.13 Long-Term Trend in Relative Performance of High Beta

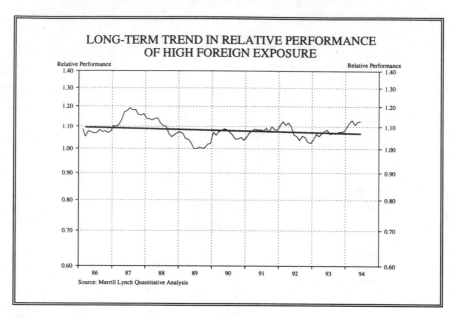

Figure 11.14 Long-Term Trend in Relative Performance of High Foreign Exposure

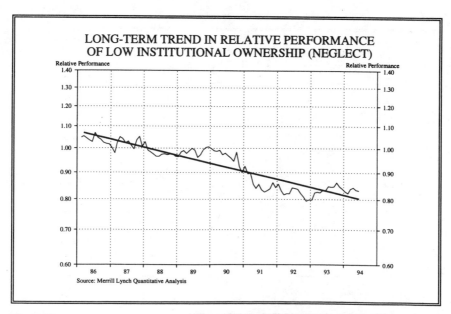

Figure 11.15 Long-Term Trend in Relative Performance of Low Institutional Ownership

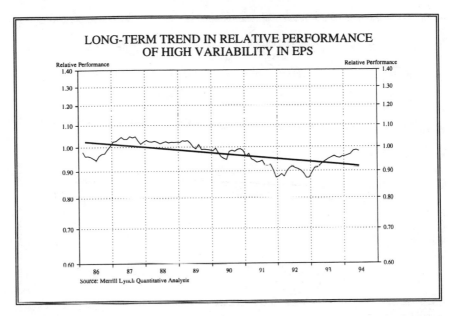

Figure 11.16 Long-Term Trend in Relative Performance of High Variability of EPS

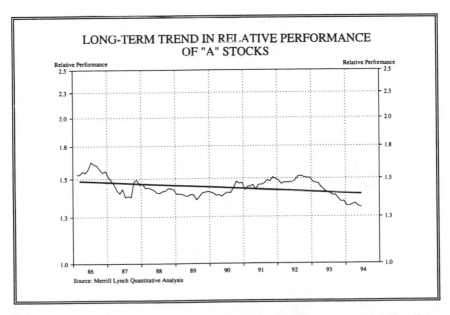

Figure 11.17 Long-Term Trend in Relative Performance of A Stocks

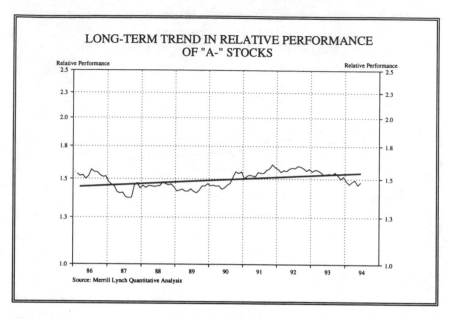

Figure 11.18   Long-Term Trend in Relative Performance of A− Stocks

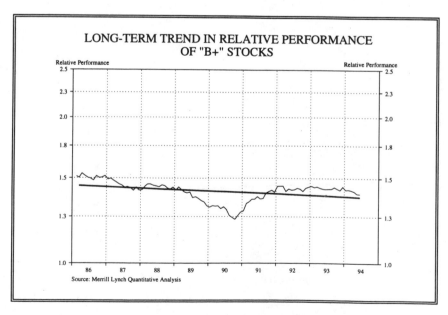

Figure 11.19   Long-Term Trend in Relative Performance of B+ Stocks

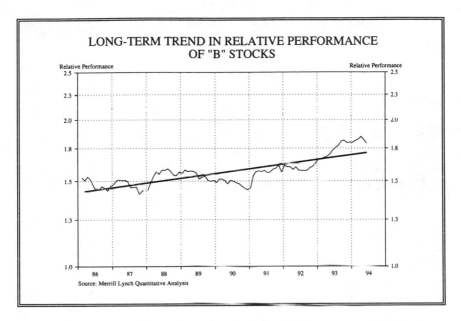

Figure 11.20 Long-Term Trend in Relative Performance of B Stocks

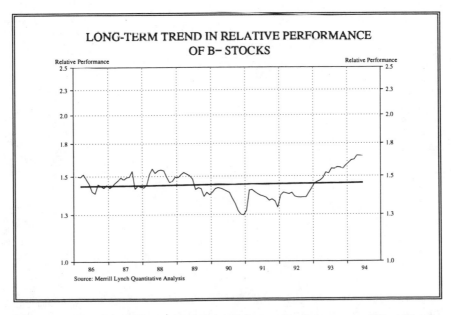

Figure 11.21 Long-Term Trend in Relative Performance of B— Stocks

most sound long-term strategy, you can bet it is time to find a new long-term strategy.

◆ References

Bernstein, Richard and Pradhuman, Satya D. "Long-Term Performance Trends." *Merrill Lynch Quantitative Viewpoint*, July 12, 1994.

Speidell, Lawrence S. "Embarrassment and Riches: The Discomfort of Alternative Investment Strategies." *Journal of Portfolio Management*, Fall 1990, pp. 6–11.

Index

P
Pension Benefit Guarantee
   Corporation (PBGC),
   171–72
Pension consultants, ix, 46,
   170, 173
   and style investing, 3–4
   See also Managers of funds;
   Style investing
Pension funds
public, 172
   volatility of, 178–79
   See also Risk
Perold, Andre, 146
Perpetuity, 125
Peters, Donald, 177
P/E-to-growth strategies, 177
Plan sponsors
   implications for, 168–90
   See also Growth funds;
   Managers of funds;
   Pension consultants; Value
   funds
Positive earnings surprise
   models, 32–33
Positive earnings surprises, 32
Pradhuman, Satya D., 10, 149,
   153–54, 157, 162, 179–80,
   185–86, 216–17
Productivity, 19, 21
Put options, 192, 196–99, 212

R
Ratings
   drift, 79
   See also Standard & Poor's,
   Common Stock Ratings

Regional small stocks
   performances, 163
Regret aversion, 92–93, 94
Research
   See Investment research
Return neutrality, 145
Risk
   aversion to, 92–93
   and character of a stock, 11,
   74
   definition of, 82, 99, 181,
   185
   duration, 12
   of equity derivatives, 194–95
   firm-specific, 100–101
   by growth sector
   classification, 105–6
   high beta versus low beta,
   97–119
   by interest rate sensitivity,
   107
   market-related, 101
   by market segment, 117
   non-diversifiable, 100–101
   perception, 26
   and performance of stock, 1,
   7, 8, 13, 74, 82–83, 110,
   112, 179
   and return relationships,
   179–87
   risk/return characteristics by
   market capitalization, 149,
   159
   Sharpe ratio (ratio of return
   to risk), 149
   See also Bankruptcy, risk of
Risk adjusted returns, 170–71